W9-CUF-099

SUDDENLY
SINGLE

How to transition into the single life
and live it successfully

KATHEY BATEY

What people are saying about

SUDDENLY **SINGLE**

"Kathey Batey is the friend the newly single need so they can work through the pain and create a new life. Kathey has walked her talk. Her book is a wonderful blend of practical advice and powerful questions, exercises and processes to get your life back on track. I just wish I knew Kathey and had her book when I became suddenly single! It would have saved me a lot of time and tears."

- Judy Anderson
Relating to Success coach and speaker

"Its time is now and its message is relevant and purposeful."

- Jane Helmstead
Licensed Professional Counselor

"Accept Suddenly Single as a wonderful guidebook to help you navigate through the loneliness, anger, hurt, and confusion on your passage to reclaiming your life! Kathey doesn't shy away from addressing the tough issues that singles face. She shares the message that life is not over when you find yourself suddenly single, you've begun a new life adventure that you hadn't planned. I can't wait to put Suddenly Single into the hands of many of my coaching clients who desperately need it!"

- Christine Schaap
Author of Bring It On! Women Embracing Midlife

"Based on my many years of working with newly single people, I've found this book, Suddenly Single to be the best resource for people rebuilding their lives. Kathey Batey covers all the necessary topics of transition, healing and the vital ingredients for starting a new life."

- Susan Zimmerman-President
Passages Transition Center

Published by Spirited Presentations

SpiritedPresentations.com

To contact Kathey Batey email: Kathey@spiritedpresentations.com

Or write:

Kathey Batey

Spirited Presentations

PO BOX 150286

Grand Rapids, MI 49515

© 2007 Kathey Batey

All rights reserved. No part of this book may be reproduced or
transmitted by any means without written permission of the publisher,
Spirited Presentations

Cover/book design by Adam Mikrut [Mikrut Design] mikrutdesign.com

ISBN: 978-0-9790017-2-7

Printed in the United States of America 2007

THIS BOOK IS DEDICATED

TO: Those who find themselves suddenly single and the potential of their future, whether they can see it or not.

TO: The God of second chances, who believes in us more than we believe in ourselves.

"Do not call to mind the former things, or ponder things of the past. Behold, I will do something new, now it will spring forth; will you not be aware of it? I will even make a roadway in the wilderness, Rivers in the desert."

Isaiah 43: 18-19

ACKNOWLEDGEMENTS

- My sincere appreciation to Leslie Charles, my editor, whose skillful hands guided my manuscript. If you were to ask me, could I have written this book without her, I would say yes. But it would hardly be worth the read. I am indebted to her patience, vision and perseverance in making this book possible.

- A big thank you to my readers, whose opinons I value – Sharon, Claire, Sheryl, Shelly, Robin, Fred, Bob, Ron, Ben, Jane.

- I am grateful to my children who believed in me no matter what. If ever I wonder what matters in this crazy world, I think of you. Thank you for your love and support.

CONTENTS

A personal note from the author

Why would I choose to write a book about transitioning into the single life? It's because I intimately understand the upheaval of suddenly becoming single. Now, years later, I realize this crisis is a passage and not a final destination. There is a new life on the other side of this crisis, and it can be a very good one. Although it may be difficult to believe at this moment, I assure you there is life after this rough transition.

The passage of becoming single is unplanned, and it holds many unknowns. My passage was certainly unplanned, when after twenty years of marriage I found myself single. I understand the feelings of loneliness, abandonment, betrayal, rejection and insecurity that accompany this life-altering event. It's not that family and friends didn't support me, they did. It's just that they could not reach the place where I hurt the most.

I wish there had been a guidebook for the transition, to give me hope and to help me understand all that I was going through; the shock of confusion, indignation, fear and pain. I needed a practical approach for redesigning my new life of being single.

In your hands is the guidebook I wished for when I suddenly became single. I know it will help you move forward, from the point of crisis to the process of healing, to find a successful life as a single person.

There is no prince or princess charming at the end of this book; that is not the answer to a new life. The wisdom here is much richer, because it allows you to gain strength within as you venture into this new territory. The treasure of this book is posed in this question: are you searching for the perfect mate or are you seeking for the perfect self, and peace within that self? Before searching elsewhere, you and I must first find our own answer to this question.

This book is ready for you when you are. We will look at this transition for what it is, a powerful time that will change your life forever. It is possible to make this transition a good one.

I recommend that you read this book with a pen in hand. Feel free to make notes upon the sidelines of the pages and journal some of your thoughts. If you prefer not to write in the book, begin a separate journal of your journey to document your thoughts and your progress as you read through the book. The ideas, questions, and single thoughts to consider will guide you through the process. You have an incredible need right now to express the emotions and thoughts you're going through. It will be part of your healing. Make this book, or your journal, a safe place to vent your losses, feelings, hopes, fears and visions for the future. You may begin this experience focused on your loss, but you will finish the story focused with determination to create a new successful life.

I want to acknowledge and honor the fact that marriage is a holy communion. It is not my intention to dishonor marriage or encourage divorce. But should divorce occur, this book is guidance for those who must go through it to find a better understanding of themselves at this critical time of transition.

Chapter 1

When I Suddenly Became Single

Every person who has become suddenly single has a unique, personal story to tell. While there are many differences between coping with divorce and enduring the loss of a loved one through death, there are also parallels that bring us to where we are today, in the world of one and suddenly single. In many ways, my experiences will be familiar to you and your situation. I hope you find a connection and a source of comfort during this difficult time. Our stories mark the beginning of our passage, starting with shock, pain or guilt, and progressing to understanding, acceptance and growth. Although your story now may be of grief and pain, you can finish your transition healed, strong, vibrant, and ready to embrace life again.

If you are in the beginning stage, I promise you won't stay there. If you've been transitioning into single life for a while, you'll find the principles of this book true and reaffirming to your own story. Come with me as you transition into the single life and learn to live it successfully. Going through this passage will transport you to a destination that can be better than you've imagined.

My Story

My story of suddenly becoming single started tragically, with my impending divorce. When my husband announced that he was leaving, the shock and the pain I felt really defies words. It felt as if someone had destroyed my life's work. His leaving felt so hurtful and unjust, to both me and our children, and that injustice sent me reeling. For me, especially early in the crisis, I learned how essential it was to talk about the injustice and pain to a counselor, friends, the air around me, or in meditation and prayer. I desperately needed to deal with, and get the injustice barb out of me.

How Did We Get Here?

The end of the relationship caused me to face the reality of the past compared to the contrast of its beginning, wondering how did we get here. Looking back, and being totally honest with myself, I now recognize our relationship grew into an unhealthy relationship with several areas of neglect. We were two people who grew so far apart that we were living independent of each other, not tending to each other, and not honoring each other the way we should have. We were too busy, too preoccupied because the relationship lacked, or was it what caused the relationship to lack? Whichever came first, because of the neglect, the relationship between us withered and died. The times we connected were rare. I now recognize the emptiness of our relationship. Like many couples we went on for years, living together while leading separate lives.

I thought what many of us secretly think: "if I work hard enough to compensate for what this relationship lacks, if I am good enough, eventually things will work out." Did you also hope that your mate would one day wake up and realize how much they have? Sadly, many times they don't see it and nothing changes. In my marriage, we woke up one morning and found our marriage dead. I'm just not sure which morning it was.

Life is too short to dwell on regrets. I am determined not to. Instead, I'll take the life lessons I learned. Many of those experiences and lessons shaped who I am today. While my relationship was often empty and lacking, I won't ever regret that it existed, or that I invested twenty years into it. Because I cannot change the past, I can only learn from it. And it is important to see the good parts and what good things did indeed come as a result of our union.

We were blessed with life's most precious gifts: two daughters and one son. My children are three of the

"Life is too short to dwell on regrets. I am determined not to. Instead, I'll take the life lessons I learned. Many of those experiences and lessons shaped who I am today. I cannot change the past, I can only learn from it."

most incredible people I've ever known. Had my life been different I would be without them, and my heart pains at the thought. At this time in my life, they are three of my most precious friends, along with their families.

Unspoken Expectations

We all have our own ideas of what we want a relationship to be. All of us carry expectations and live according to them, or we struggle, determined to make life live up to our expectations. In my marriage, it was our unexpressed expectations that made it impossible for us to truly reach each other. Those expectations created a wall between us that neither of us could see or get past. We each expected something different than what our partner could give. And though we denied or failed to acknowledge their existence, our expectations were very real, and far more influential than we realized. We lacked the communication skills to express and listen to each other's needs. As with many couples, we grew apart. And in the busyness of life it didn't seem to be noticed. I knew I was unable to please him, so I gave up trying. I shut down emotionally early in the marriage, and somewhere along the way, he did too. I shut down because my vital needs were unmet, and so were my expectations. My expectations were for emotional support. It was so important to me and I realized that I had lived many, many years without it.

We were isolated people living in the same house. We both were left wanting and lonely. Now, when I'm alone at least I know I'm alone. I know where I stand. There is not the endless longing to connect, or become a beggar of spirit for a connection. For many years of my marriage, I lived life on autopilot. I tried to reach out, saw the lack of responsiveness, got discouraged and shut down. I tried to reach out, received no response, got discouraged and shut down, again and again. It was like beating my head against a brick wall. Indeed it was a wall; a wall of expectations. The cycle continued for years. I wish I could say it was unique to us, but it isn't. Do you see any similarities in your former life?

A Dose of Reality

The truth is that denial only works for a time, and reality not only shows up, but becomes blatant and unavoidable. My reality was, after one year of my husband sleeping on the couch, he wanted out of the marriage. I suppose it seems odd that I was shocked, but I was. For so many years I denied the distance between us. But deep inside, I knew I had lost respect for this man and he had none left for me. The hurt was incredible. But by facing the painful truth, reality actually brought relief. The truth, while painful and difficult to face, is actually easier to deal with than continuing to deny what is real.

"The truth, while painful and difficult to face, is actually easier to deal with than continuing to deny what is real."

The death of a mate leads you to feel rejected in many ways. You are left behind to face all of life's responsibilities alone. What was once a life shared with joys and burdens is now yours alone. That reality faces you every moment and makes the world feel so empty. It can seem surreal and such a contrast to the reality that once existed.

Three Single Thoughts to Consider
- *What emotions are most prevalent when you think of your past relationship?*
- *What unexpressed expectations existed in your relationship?*
- *In what areas was there denial, for yourself, for your partner?*

"This person you once loved in intimacy is now a stranger, a distant enemy. The lawyer calls to discuss details, and this stranger takes your spouse's place to discuss your future. How odd. How strange. How wrong."

Hitting Bottom

The moment of hitting bottom will differ for each of us, but it does come. For me, it was the day when the divorce papers came. The door closed behind my husband and I stood alone in our empty house. I fell to the bottom hitting hard with the feelings of abandonment, and feeling unreachable and totally alone on planet earth. The bottom is a dark and dreary place, and you feel like you're suffocating. You feel naked, helpless and hopeless.

For the divorced, the bottom plunges further when he comes back for his things, and he talks about dividing your life into two separate piles. This person you once loved in intimacy is now a stranger, a distant enemy. The lawyer calls to discuss details, and this stranger takes your spouse's place to discuss your future. How odd. How strange. How wrong.

If your loss is through death, your "bottom" may be your feelings of abandonment or even anger at your spouse for leaving you behind, even though you know he or she didn't want or choose to go. At the bottom, you still wait for them to walk in the door. You remember the scent of his body, or her cologne is still on the clothes. Their hair is in the brush. Where did life go? This is the bottom.

I cried, like you cry. You cry and you hurt, and words and thoughts and feelings bounce off of you and inside you, all at the same time. You feel guilty, shameful, betrayed, rejected, abandoned, deceived, inadequate, isolated, loss and grief.

And if you left your mate you also feel guilty, shameful, betrayed, rejected, abandoned, deceived, inadequate, isolated, loss and grief. Your thoughts scream "how dare you," or "How dare you not be what I need you to be?" That's hitting bottom.

If you feel as if you're at the bottom now, don't give up. Hang on. The bottom is simply a part of the passage. It's a dark, dreary part of your journey, but on the other side is a future. There's a new future looming in the distance; I assure you it's there.

"If you feel as if you're at the bottom now, don't give up. Hang on. The bottom is simply a part of the passage. It's a dark, dreary part of your journey, but on the other side is a future."

If death's sting has pierced your heart, hold on. Take a deep breath. Hope will come, healing will happen. It sounds like a cliché but time does help heal your shattered heart. Your future will offer possibilities that never crossed your mind before, because you were not in a place where they could. Wrap your arms around your own soul, and hold on. Ease your hurt by accepting the support and offers of help from those who care about you.

My Survival Means You Can, Too

"No matter how dark it seems at any given moment, look for the small glimmers of hope to hold onto and they will assist you to crawl out from the bottom toward life."

Somehow, mercifully, in the midst of this darkness there was a tiny light. In the middle of all the chaos and confusion there was the spirit of survival. I began to feel that I had not truly been abandoned completely. My spirit had a Comforter that provided a sense of support I had never experienced before. Of course, I had never been in this dark place before. That tiny pinprick of light, that sense of knowing there was something beyond despair, was hope. It was just a glimmer, but as I began to slowly work my way up from the bottom, that glimmer became bigger and brighter. No matter how dark it seems at any given moment, look for the small glimmers of hope to hold onto and they will assist you to crawl out from the bottom toward life. The glimmer of hope for me is so aptly put in Pam Thumb's song, Life Is Hard:

"Life is hard, the world is cold,
you're barely young and then you're old.
Every fallen tear is always understood;
life is hard, but God is good."

For me, that tiny light was my faith, the source of hope I had built years before. The foundation of my faith had held me up in past years and was strong enough to hold me once again.

Faith allows you to survive emotional pain. It is the core belief that keeps you from being swept away by negative emotions and self-doubt. Look for, and hold on to your faith to find solid ground.

Anchor yourself within the faith you have, because your emotions will run the gamut. From moments of hope to moments of despair, you will have times of confidence and times of fear. You also will have moments of insight, moments of acceptance and moments of anger. Your heart may feel as if every touch of human kindness is like a cooling stroke to your burning flesh. Your brain may feel numb, yet it will grab onto every note of every soulful song you hear.

"The transition from marriage to singleness is a strange time, and it is a powerful time. In fact, I am convinced it is one of life's most powerful times."

A Time of Power and Pain

The transition from marriage to singleness is a strange time, and it is a powerful time. In fact, I am convinced it is one of life's most powerful times, because you become hypersensitive to your experiences. It can be perilous or productive, rich with lessons and insights, or ignored to your detriment. Pay attention to the experience and learn from it. Take advantage of the opportunities that can help stabilize you by seeking help or counseling, talking to close friends, or journaling your thoughts and struggles.

Take good care of yourself during this time. Be aware of the choices you make and the people you let into your life and heart. Support yourself by making sure you avoid negative thinking, such as "I don't care," or "nothing matters now." It is normal to rationalize or justify self-defeating behaviors when you are going through a crisis and facing depression. Understand that this too will pass. You matter – you matter greatly. This is not a final destination. The fog will clear and the hurt will lessen. You can and will feel whole again.

"If death's sting has pierced your heart, hold on. Take a deep breath. Hope will come; healing will happen. Wrap your arms around your own soul, and hold on."

Just Plain Messy

Divorces are messy. There are few clean-cut endings to a marriage relationship. Typically, there are awkward attempts at getting back together. There are false starts and stops, and hopes for reconciliation along the way. Sometimes the very thing we hope for happens, but it's often too little, too late. On the day my divorce was supposed to be final, my husband called, stating that he wanted reconciliation. He wanted our family back together again. I embraced the move, and I embraced him.

He did come back, to the same world he left. We still lacked the ability to communicate. The wall of expectations stood impenetrable between us. The marriage counselor was right; we were ten years too late. Five days after he came back, my husband left again. Hitting bottom for the second time was even deeper than the first. It was darker and colder than before. Maybe it was because this time I knew it really was the end. I had given my marriage one more chance, only to see it fail again. I gave it one more chance because there was a lot at stake, the future of my precious family, and the rest of my life.

Standing in the kitchen, feeling helpless, I asked God to hold me. "Just hold me," that's all I could utter. In the quiet of that afternoon, He did. And I know in your search for strength and comfort, if you are at the bottom for the first or the second time, you can find what you need. At that moment, God will hold you. To accept this, is to have the hope to begin healing.

Giving it the final effort and another chance actually allowed closure for me. I knew I had put forth the final attempt to save my marriage. This sense of closure gave me strength, and when the offer for reconciliation came again, I said no. I had given the marriage the honor

"Standing in the kitchen, feeling helpless, I asked God to hold me. "Just hold me," that's all I could utter. In the quiet of that afternoon, He did."

it deserved, the final chance to make things work. This was a turning point for me. I gained strength and dignity by setting boundaries around the value of my own soul and how I would allow myself and my family to be treated. It helped me find closure and protection for myself against further abuse and hurt.

Boundaries of Protection

I understood the offense to my soul was a spiritual issue. By setting boundaries of self-preservation, I determined once and for all what was acceptable, whom I would open myself up to, and whom I would trust. This man became an unsafe person for me, because he did not love me, nor care for my future. I could not control his action, only my reaction. Setting boundaries was a huge first step forward for me. The decision to say "no" gave me strength to continue, to have the power to move forward, to find my way out of the darkness at the bottom. This turning point was not the end of my turmoil, but it was the end of my confusion on the subject. By establishing healthy boundaries, I created a respect for myself. I didn't allow myself to focus on rejection and all the second-guessing that comes with it: "Why wasn't I good enough? What's the matter with me? Why was I so unworthy of being loved?" Those lies were replaced with God's hope.

Recovering from loss after divorce or a loved one's

"Setting boundaries was a huge first step forward for me. The decision to say "no" gave me strength to continue, to have the power to move forward, to find my way out of the darkness at the bottom."

death means facing a time of challenge and difficulty. It requires you to define your value, and redefine who you are by what you allow into your life. Once your personal boundaries are in place, you have defined your value and level of self-respect. Give yourself hope by determining your boundaries, your mindset, and your message. "I will not allow you to treat me this way. I will respect and value myself. I will set boundaries. I will take power over my own life." See your value, recognize what is harmful to you, and do not allow it into your life.

Realize you have the right not to respond, discuss, or argue the details. Don't allow yourself to get dragged into arguing or fighting. In the past, you may have felt obligated to respond to every question, every process, every detail, but life's rules have just changed. You don't have to figure everything out, other than what directly affects you and the children. This is for your protection and the children's too. Know when to hold onto hope for this relationship, but equally important, know when to shut off the discussion.

How do you determine your boundaries and a healthy mindset? Start by refusing to become the victim. The first step is not to let your emotions overwhelm you or paralyze you. Make the decision to go beyond the injustice or bitterness. If you choose to stay and dwell on the negatives you become a powerless victim. There is nothing

"How do you determine your boundaries and a healthy mindset? Start by refusing to become the victim. The first step is not to let your emotions overwhelm you or paralyze you."

good in being a victim. Because in truth, if you choose to be the victim, there is not a rescuer for you. You will see some individuals who live with a sword sticking out of their heart for years, even a lifetime. They show and tell the wounds over and over again for years. People can get stuck in the injustice instead of taking the steps toward healing. This is something you must do for yourself. Come up from the bottom to explore what is now possible in your life that wasn't possible before.

Three Single Thoughts to Consider
- *What boundaries did you have in this past relationship?*
- *What boundaries have you set for those around you?*
- *What is your mindset at this moment? Do you see some glimmer of hope?*

"Come up from the bottom to explore what is now possible in your life that wasn't possible before."

Finding Hope to Hold Onto

Hope can come from others. When it comes, hold it fervently. I was reminded of this many times while going through my divorce. In one of my moments of despair, my wise and beautiful friend Dorothy looked me in the eye with determination and said, "Kathey, you're going to be all right." It sounded so simple, but to me, her reassurance was profound. Her words brought hope to my dismal, hurting heart. Another time, a wonderful pastor came up to me and asked a question I will remember all of my life. He asked,

"How can I pray for you?" He gave no words of advice, no judgment, just understanding and love that I needed so much. It is so like the Jesus I know. Listen to those tender giving words people extend to you and savor them, accept them, and don't let them pass by unnoticed. Let your mind wrap around them and allow them to minister to you.

In the middle of your struggles, you will receive moments of love and caring that will ease your aching heart. God bless the people who are compassionate enough to care for you in time of tragedy. There will be people who cross your path and give you what you need. Keep your eye open for them. Because you will need words of encouragement, kind deeds and a compassionate touch. This may be the first time you have ever had to reach out in need. You must allow yourself to do so, even if you've never asked for help before. Receiving help, support, or comfort from others may feel awkward, but it's necessary. Accepting other people's kindness allows them to give. It also allows you to be more understanding when, in the future, someone reaches out to you in their time of need.

Divorce and death can hurt deeply. While facilitating divorce recovery groups, I have witnessed some amazing moments. I've seen men and women, regardless of their position in life, from CEOs to stay at home Moms, break down and sob like little children. Some people allow themselves to reach out and not be alone at this critical

"Listen to those tender giving words people extend to you and savor them, accept them, and don't let them pass by unnoticed. Let your mind wrap around them and allow them to minister to you."

time. It's difficult to be so vulnerable, yet it helps us recover. No one wants to feel vulnerable or needy. All of us will face tough times in our lives, no matter how strong or determined we are. Death and divorce are the great leveler of humanity. Right now, review the list of people who are there for you. Then ask yourself who you know that you could reach out to. Most likely, they're the people who will support you in your time of need.

You will be surprised at how compassionate some people's comments are. You also may be disappointed in the actions or reactions of those you thought were close friends. This is a defining moment for many relationships. Please understand that family and friends are trying to process this major event too. We all perceive loss and change differently, and some simply don't know how to react. If they wish to withdraw or remain silent, let them do so. Your truest friends will rise to the occasion. They are the ones you will cherish for a lifetime. Similar to what happens at a funeral, some people will say and do some strange things. Chances are they want to help, but don't know how. Forgive them. Don't waste your energy worrying about what others think or say or how they react. You will need all your energy for yourself and for your kids. You also will need energy for counseling, if you decide to go that route.

Even though divorce is commonplace today, it is still a great tragedy of loss. Certainly the tearing of flesh is

"Death and divorce are the great leveler of humanity. Right now, review the list of people who are there for you. Then ask yourself who you know that you could reach out to."

the best illustration. Since when we do marry, we become one flesh, emotionally, spiritually, and financially. When the flesh tears, everyone is affected; the children, friends, the extended family. Your community is emotionally wounded and the family tree will never be the same.

Three Single Thoughts to Consider
- *Who has supported you during this time?*
- *Who has disappointed you?*
- *Who has exceeded your expectations?*

Reclaiming Your Future

Living one day at a time may sound trite, but it is so true. In the depth of my pain, I couldn't look too far into the future - it felt overwhelming and terrifying to do so. For my own sanity I had to slow life down and focus on each day. Sometimes I could only focus on an hour at a time to survive. I had to ask myself simple questions like:

Can I get out of bed this morning?
Do I need to take this day off?
Can I muster the energy to take a shower?
Can I get the kids their lunch money, or remind them of their ride arrangements for sports?
Do I need to sit down, or do I simply need to cry?"
I would touch my face, my shoulders, just for the sensation;

just to remind myself that I was in fact still alive.

Like a frightening roller coaster ride, many of my early days were shaky, scary, and unpredictable. I would find that I was holding my breath and then I needed to encourage myself. I lived moment by moment, reminding myself to breathe, to hold onto the rail, to know this out-of-control ride would soon end. My biggest fear was that I would become paralyzed by overwhelming questions that had no answers;

How did it come to this?
Can I do this?
What will happen to me?
What's on the other side?
Do I have the strength to make it on my own?

"This emotional roller-coaster ride does eventually come to an end. It is not a sudden stop, nor an early one, but I promise you it's there."

This emotional roller-coaster ride does eventually come to an end. It is not a sudden stop, nor an early one, but I promise you it's there.

Three Single Thoughts to Consider:
- *What is your biggest fear right now?*
- *Where are you finding strength to get through the days?*
- *What is the best thing you are doing for yourself to get through this time?*

Every divorce story is unique. I shared a part of mine in the hope that it in some way parallels your story. If you feel betrayal as your number one emotion, I must also tell you that I understand that emotion. I have met with the drama, the abandonment, the betrayal of an affair, and the humiliating stories that followed. Whatever your story, I know what you are going through and I understand the pain. Whether you were the one to leave, or you were left behind, you hurt in many of the same ways I have. Right now, in the middle of this, it's impossible not to hurt.

There has to be a turning point from the pain and I hope you're ready to make the turn. Now is the time to get started on the future, on the process of becoming single. In the coming chapters we will look at finding support, making good decisions, starting over, taking risks (and even enjoying them), nurturing existing relationships, and starting new ones. Becoming suddenly single can be miserable or it can be glorious. You can help yourself through this difficult (and rewarding) process if you are honestly willing to look inside and allow yourself time to grieve and heal.

"There has to be a turning point from the pain and I hope you're ready to make the turn. Now is the time to get started on the future, on the process of becoming single. "

Chapter 2

Grieving and Healing

Only the strong person is brave enough to grieve, to measure his loss, and to then let it go.

Coping Techniques

The experience of divorce or the death of a partner is like an earthquake, the ground is trembling and we feel like we are falling. We will instinctively reach out for something to hold onto to sustain us that will help us find our balance from the trembling ground, a grip to begin to grieve our way through it.

Our methods may be healthy or unhealthy. We will focus on the healthy methods that are effective and truly allow us to heal. Even though the unhealthy methods might temporarily mask the pain, they are neither long lasting, nor effective. There are numerous techniques you will use (or see others use) to get through this tough time.

A coping skill is a technique or strategy used to get us through a crisis. It is not the answer to the problem. It

"A coping skill is a technique or strategy used to get us through a crisis. It is not the answer to the problem. It is the method we use to tolerate, overcome, or maybe even avoid the problem."

is the method we use to tolerate, overcome, or maybe even avoid the problem. It's natural to use a coping mechanism for a time. Unfortunately, it doesn't correct the problem, it just helps get us through it.

Healthy Coping Skills	Unhealthy Coping Skills
Self-nurturing behavior	Little food/excessive food
Healing music	Excessive drink
Prayer/scripture	Anger
Self-help books	Withdrawal
Journaling	Defeating self talk
Counseling	Excessive shopping
Talking with safe people	Workaholism
Planning for the future	Inability to work
	Depression

"It's natural to use a coping mechanism for a time. Unfortunately, it doesn't correct the problem, it just helps get us through it."

Here are some of the coping methods I've relied on. Perhaps you can relate to some of them.

Tears. Allowing time to cry sounds obvious, but you may find like I did that you have stuffed your emotions for survival purposes and "keeping the stiff upper lip" for those around you. You must allow yourself the time and energy to truly grieve. Grieving will honor the relationship and the loss. Tears are designed to release and remove toxins from the body. Crying can bring great relief, physically and spiritually. Tears can help you to let it go. Not only did you earn those tears, you need them to release your hurt instead of holding onto it.

Finding Comfort. Seek ways that comfort you. This coping mechanism may seem crazy but I found comfort sleeping with my dog - Sadie. Sadie was a one hundred pound Rottweiler. Desperate means called for desperate measures, I suppose. Yes, I slept with her, and no dog got more hugging than she did. Sadie was a big baby and she loved it. Hugging my dog saved a few of my friends a bit of extra emotional wear and tear, and I needed the furry support.

Music. I listened to endless hours of country music videos, "man left, dog died, woe is my life in this pickup truck," type of stuff. Although not my usual choice of music, I could relate to those lyrics. All that hand wringing and heart twanging allowed me something I could connect with. Country music worked for me during the grieving process, yet, I rarely listen to it today.

Why Coping Mechanisms Work

We seek these techniques to find comfort and the attempt to rebalance our lives. We may decide to run wild to avoid the pain, to show that we're still young and vibrant. We might drink to dull the sharpness of the details of this crisis.

These self-indulgent techniques work for a while,

but when you get sober, or are faced with the bills from your spree, it won't bring you closer to peace, but a greater distance away from it. Why further complicate your already complicated life?

Three Single Thoughts to Consider
- *What healthy coping techniques are you using right now?*
- *What unhealthy coping mechanisms do you most need to avoid?*
- *What new coping strategies might you want to consider?*

Coping by Replacing

There is one unwise decision many people make to cope with the loss of a life mate or partner. They try as quickly as possible to replace the mate. They will get into a new relationship before they are ready. Understandably, it is during a crisis that you need comfort the most. This is a natural and legitimate need. You may be vulnerable enough right now that it's tempting to seek comfort in the arms of the opposite sex. Some people may say, what's wrong with that? Well, for one, you cannot think clearly or comprehend fully right now the ramifications of a new relationship. I know this because I was there. During this period of vulnerability, you will have a lot on your mind. Your head (like my head at the time) is not on straight right now. You can easily make the wrong decisions, like believing you are falling in love with someone when you're not healed yet, or moving in with or marrying someone before you're strong, healthy and ready. That will only hurt you and the person you are using as your coping outlet.

I look back at the first man I dated after the divorce, and ask myself now, what was I thinking? I was not thinking clearly. He would have never been the mate for me for many reasons. But I needed someone to value me, to hold me. He was my healing relationship. My ex thought I could do nothing right, this man thought I could do nothing wrong. I desperately needed that kind of unconditional adoration and regard but sadly, it wasn't enough to base a whole relationship on.

The healing relationship occurs because you desperately need someone to make you feel whole again. You desperately need someone who believes in you, someone who thinks you're wonderful, and someone to hold you. The relationship cannot be honest, because your heart is not ready. You need a warm body to fill the void in your life that is so enormous. You hang on because it feels so good, and you need it so much.

In my healing relationship, it was healing because it was the opposite of where I came from. Where my husband was critical, I was now adored. Where he walked away as I exposed my feelings, this man listened intently to my feelings. This man helped me see my value. I soaked

"The healing relationship occurs because you desperately need someone to make you feel whole again. "

it up like a sponge, but I was too hurt to be in an honest relationship; I was too needy and not truly healed. Because the healing relationship is for your healing, it may take advantage of the other person. Consider the person who will hold you out of water just long enough for you to catch your breath so you won't drown. Eventually, he or she will no longer be able to hold you up. That is the unhealthy part. Chances are, the person you are in the healing relationship with is the one you will end up hurting. Why? Because this person may have unrealistic expectations for this relationship; and because you are not you right now, and you are not who you will be when this transition is over.

God bless them for being there as they hold you out of the water, but while you survive because of them, they may drown in the process. It is a difficult time for both of you. This is one of the many reasons that you have to heal before going into a new relationship.

"You must take care of your old business before you are ready to start anything new, so proceed with caution on the first relationship after the divorce or the death of your mate."

You must take care of your old business before you are ready to start anything new, so proceed with caution on the first relationship after the divorce or the death of your mate. Keep your eyes wide open and continually examine your own heart and make sure the reason you need the relationship is not solely to ease the pain you feel.

Three Single Thoughts to Consider

- *How long has it been since your divorce or the death of your partner?*
- *Do you consider yourself ready for a new relationship?*

• *List three expectations you have for your new relationship*

Coping by Rescuing Everybody Else

To cope with all the demands of your situation, you may temporarily slip into rescuer mode as a coping technique to spare your children as much grief as possible and to assure yourself that life can be normal. You may feverishly try to keep everything running as close to normal as possible. As a self-appointed savior, you try to make up for everything to those around you. You overcompensate in several ways, the physical and the emotional by buying things or trying to fill in the roles of the other parent. This is done with the intent of shielding others from hurt, saving the day and minimizing the disruption as much as possible.

As a part of the savior mode, you may try to save the relationship between your spouse and the children. The truth is, each parent has to save or maintain their own relationship with the children, and the children also have to be willing to save it. Children are smart, they see the truth inevitably and they know deep down they will have to deal with it. Unfortunately, you can't save it. You can certainly offer some stability by being strong in your own relationship with the children. You can spare them unnecessary heartache by not bashing your ex-spouse. Consider that every negative word you speak goes directly to their sensitive heart that is already hurting from this incredible personal loss in their life and the foundation of their life. Assist your children in healing by being honest with the amount of information their age and maturity can handle. You will heal faster by realizing you cannot save the other parent and child's relationship. You can act as a buffer, but you cannot eradicate the hurt completely. Ask them their thoughts on counseling, or ask them whom they are talking to about what is happening in their life. They need someone other than you who will listen. Watch for opportunities to gently guide them through their crisis. Refrain from providing all the solutions, allow them to talk.

"Watch for opportunities to gently guide them through their crisis. Refrain from providing all the solutions, allow them to talk."

Grieving Through Communication

The best thing you can do right now is to keep the communication lines open, so you are there emotionally and physically for your kids as much as possible. And then, make sure you are. Be as honest as possible and explain only as much as their age can handle. Hold them tight, especially teenagers, and honestly tell them how sorry you are that they hurt. Tell them that you hurt because they hurt. Acknowledge how difficult this must be for them. Speak your words gently and without anger or emotion toward your ex. It can be so powerful when you say it without emotion. Your presence of mind and acceptance will help ease your children into their new reality.

If you are the one who chose to leave, hold your

kids especially tight. Reassure them of their value to you. Reassure your children that it is not their fault daddy or mommy is moving out, and they are the most special people in the world to both of you. Don't be afraid to state the obvious. Don't just say I love you, define what that means. Dig deep here. It's necessary to explain your heart and not leave your children to their own assumptions. Allowing them to talk and grieve will help them heal and move on, so they don't have to play out this loss the rest of their lives.

The difficult part is not to lean on your children through this process. Consider a qualified counselor, pastor or friend for the children as well as yourself. Having an outsider to talk to will help all of you so you don't lean on your children, and they get a more objective view of what they are going through. It is too great a burden to place on them. It's unfair to impose adult burdens on those small shoulders, even if they are teenagers or grown children. They have their own grief to deal with and they are processing it the best way they know how. Reassure them of their precious value and that nothing they did led to the divorce.

"The difficult part is not to lean on your children through this process. Consider a qualified counselor, pastor or friend for the children as well as yourself. "

Four Single Thoughts to Consider
- *How well are your children dealing with this divorce or death?*

- *Who else are they talking to besides you, and is that person a healthy influence?*
- *How are you helping your children to cope through this loss?*
- *Are you finding quiet time to talk with your children or keeping up the normal pace?*

Friends are Great Coping Sources

I found that friends were my best coping outlet. I will forever be indebted to the women who listened to me. As I went through the divorce I learned to have girlfriends again. I had become withdrawn and dutiful as a wife, never realizing how much power and healing can be in relationships with girlfriends. There were the 4 D's: Dorothy, Darcy, Darla, Diane and then Eva. They started out as co-workers and ended up as dear friends. The greatest thing they did for me was to listen. I will never underestimate the power of listening again.

Dorothy was the woman of wisdom. Darla and Darcy were the comical and compassionate ones who, having been divorced, gave me moments of relief in laughter and understanding. I took the risk of making myself vulnerable by expressing my emotions. My friends acknowledged and substantiated my feelings. Not every woman can be a girlfriend, but when you find one you will realize how vital they are. They listened and most

"I found that friends were my best coping outlet. I will forever be indebted to the women who listened to me. The greatest thing they did for me was to listen. I will never underestimate the power of listening again."

importantly, they were true friends who did not judge.

They threw me the greatest surprise party when I turned 40, the same year my divorce was final. These friends literally helped me survive. They had no idea how special they were to me. Do not underestimate the importance of same sex relationships. For me, I will never be without girlfriends again. I will cherish and nurture these relationships because I know how important they are to my sanity.

Be aware of your coping outlets, and if they are beneficial. Finding healthy distractions allow us a break from the pain, and have their purpose. We need to look away from the intensity of the situation. But as you use your own coping techniques, don't deny the fact that they are not the answer. The answer is working through the emotions of this time.

"Finding healthy distractions allow us a break from the pain, and have their purpose. We need to look away from the intensity of the situation."

Four Single Thoughts to Consider
- *Are you able to be brutally honest with yourself and about your feelings?*
- *Are you willing to open up to someone to work through this loss?*
- *Do you have a safe person to grieve with so you can let it go?*
- *If you don't find yourself currently blessed with loving*

friends, have you considered counseling or finding someone whom you can reach out to as a healthy sounding board?

Finding a Counselor

Some people are able to privately work through their own loss and process their grief. For others, counseling has proven to be very helpful, in fact, it will speed up the process of healing substantially. Maybe it's time to ask yourself if counseling would be right for you. Counselors are trained to ask the kinds of questions that will give you insight and healing strength for the rest of your life. We all have blind spots, regardless of how emotionally intelligent we may be.

For me, counseling was very beneficial. Questions presented to me helped me seek out answers and discover things that were stuck inside of me. Some were difficult to face and well hidden. The right question brings to mind the depth of what is hurting us. Good questions help us discover how we've been hurt and what decisions were made to cope with that pain, loss or disappointment. Counseling is hard work, but by bringing out all that's hidden in our hurts, we can neutralize it. Stuffing our hurt inside, denying its power is unhealthy, and unfortunately, our unresolved pain still surfaces in dramatic ways that sneak up on us physically and emotionally.

"Counselors are trained to ask the kinds of questions that will give you insight and healing strength for the rest of your life. We all have blind spots, regardless of how emotionally intelligent we may be."

What Can You expect from a Counselor?

Questions, lots of questions. You can expect to dig deep into areas and subjects you think do not relate. You can expect to cover topics that are not comfortable. The process takes time. Counseling is not a fast, magic pill that resolves the issues, but it is worth the investment. It is worth opening yourself up to it.

What Can You Expect from Yourself?

Counseling is hard work. You will sometimes feel drained at the end of a session. But it can be cleansing to deal with uncomfortable emotions and explore territory you have never tread upon before. How else will you release all that weighs upon your shoulders and within your heart? Your emotions have to go somewhere. Let them out in a safe, supportive environment. It is so much better for your physical and emotional health. You must take care of old business before you can start anew.

Good counselors will help you work through anger, resentment and dealing with business of the past, so that you can start your new path. You could literally save many tears and years by seeking professional help. There are also some wonderful programs that are in group settings such as DivorceCare®. Through support groups, you will find like-minded people who are going through the same experience who empathize with where you are. You will see that you are not alone in your experience.

"Stuffing our hurt inside, denying its power is unhealthy, and unfortunately, our unresolved pain still surfaces in dramatic ways that sneak up on us physically and emotionally."

Dealing with Anger

Anger is a natural response to emotional pain. The question is what will you do with your anger? Even if it is justified it can be potentially dangerous if you don't know how to channel it. There may be the fire of anger raging inside of you that, if kept inside, will burn you. You need to release your anger by letting it go in a healthy manner. Talking it through can diffuse it. Vocalize it as you grapple with the injustice that has created your anger. You can make the powerful decision to work through anger instead of letting anger work through you. Have you ever seen an angry person you want to be around? I haven't. After honestly dealing with anger, you will be better able to take an inventory of what is right and good in your life and start putting your energy toward building a new life instead of spending it in anger.

"Have you ever seen an angry person you want to be around? I haven't."

There was a man in my divorce recovery group who kept his head bowed during most of the session. But as we discussed the issue of anger in divorce he became animated just long enough to make the most enlightening statement. He raised his head, and carefully stated, "Of course I'm angry. If I'm not angry, then I have to face the pain. Anger is my only defense - the only way I know how to protect myself." Anger is a natural defense. However, it is necessary to face the pain and resolve the anger. You can only deny it, avoid it, or mask it for so long, at some point you have to deal with it. But it's also the best way to get the anger out.

Divorce sparks anger, and often, so does the death of your spouse. If death of your mate is how you became suddenly single, you may feel that life has stolen the most precious part of your future. When something is stolen, we feel injustice and anger. You may find yourself directing your anger to all the wrong places and people and even toward yourself. Open conversations and therapy may be necessary to face all that comes with suddenly becoming single through death. I've already stated how difficult counseling is. After all, many times, therapy is finding out what you don't want to know. But knowing and dealing with those tough issues allow you to move on with your life. You move beyond the issues, so they won't dictate the rest of your life.

In our society, it appears easier for men to deny their emotional pain. Some work it out in different ways, sometimes in unhealthy ways. I've noticed that ninety percent of the people attending the divorce recovery groups I facilitate are women. Allowing themselves to reach out for help is one way that women may fare better in dealing with divorce or death. Many women are in touch with their emotions and can lay them out on the table, and deal with them easier than men can. Women usually have a better social and emotional network to draw from. However, even women who believe they are in touch with their emotions

"Of course I'm angry. If I'm not angry, then I have to face the pain. Anger is my only defense - the only way I know how to protect myself."

will discover things that are unknown and need to be dealt with. The healthiest men I have known (and dated) are those who sought counseling. They went head on, dealing with their feelings of anger, pain, and forgiveness after their divorce, or the death of their spouse.

The Role of Forgiveness in Healing

According to Ron Nydam, Professor of Pastoral Care at Calvin College, ninety percent of pastoral therapy is forgiving the people who hurt you. Divorce, suicide, illness and betrayal are just a few. Right now it might feel impossible for you to forgive the person who left you. I am not insisting that right this minute you forgive. I am only suggesting that sometime soon, forgiveness is necessary for your own growth and survival. When you forgive anyone who has wronged you, you may also end up forgiving yourself.

"I am not insisting that right this minute you forgive. I am only suggesting that sometime soon, forgiveness is necessary for your own growth and survival."

I wish I knew whom to credit for saying this, and I hope some day I'll know. But this word picture frames it so well I must state it here "Resentment is like taking poison and expecting the other person to die" When you forgive, you free yourself. Learn to let it go. To forgive and letting it go is a part of your healing. Some feel they maintain control by withholding forgiveness. You do not gain control, in fact you lose control over your own life into the hands of anger.

There may be anger toward yourself for failure in the past relationship, which actually benefits no one, not even you. Where do you stand in your self-forgiveness? To heal completely you need to be able to forgive and leave it behind. I wrote the passage below for a dear friend who was unable to forgive himself, and he hurt terribly because of it.

I Forgive Me

I stand before God to bear my soul and mind. I am not hiding any longer. I am desperate to know peace in this moment. Standing in His graciousness and belief of His love for me, I ask Him for forgiveness of the wrong that I've willingly done. God, I am not hiding any longer. It is by faith, by my deepest heart belief that I face my failures honestly, admitting to them and I place them upon the cross of Jesus Christ. This is the only real healing place that I can go to. I ask once and for all forgiveness and freedom to let it go, so it will let go of me. I will have no peace until I do. I receive His forgiveness, I claim His mercy and power and authority to forgive. "For You Lord are good, and ready to forgive, and full of loving kindness to all who call upon You." He is the truth and the final judge and He longs to set me free. I forgive me, because He will.

Forgiveness of self allows for openness to receive a new life. Forgiveness of self dissolves guilt. Guilt does not heal us and it has no redeeming benefit. It keeps us in a self-imposed prison with the door wide open, and we are unable to walk out. I encourage you to forgive yourself as well as your spouse, and anyone else that you need to forgive. It will allow you to move on to your new life.

Guilt can be paralyzing. I have a precious friend who remains imprisoned by guilt. He is a brilliant, successful man who is an authority in his field. He literally travels the world over, lecturing on his expertise, but personally he remains depressed and unwilling to forgive himself. He seems determined to punish himself for his failed marriage. He will not get past it.

"Imagine the freedom if you surrender your right to hurt someone in revenge, and choose to let it go?"

Forgiveness of self and others is there for the asking. Is it simple? No, but when you pursue it with a sincere heart it is possible. Forgiveness is not so much for the other party as it is for you. Imagine the freedom if you surrender your right to hurt someone in revenge, and choose to let it go? Imagine the relief! If you protest this idea and feel you want to hurl this book across the room, I understand.

You may not be able to consider it yet, but in time, I urge you to be open to forgiveness if you want to heal. Because not forgiving will destroy you more than it will destroy anyone else. Give yourself that opportunity to be free. Does the sunrise every morning give you another chance? Yes it does, not for vengeance, but for vantage. For your sake I encourage you to deal with forgiveness of others and forgiveness of self. It will help you start the next glorious chapter of your life. It is part of the grieving process and vital for your healing.

Three Single Thoughts to Consider
- *Who do you most need to forgive and for what?*
- *If you were ready to relinquish the anger, resentment or revengeful feelings what would be your first step?*
- *What might your life be like if you were able to forgive and let go of your hurt?*

I consider myself very fortunate that my ex-spouse did ask my forgiveness and it gave me a certain sense of closure. Perhaps you will never hear a request for forgiveness from the one who has hurt you. What will you do with that injustice? If you have been wronged and the offender never takes responsibility for his or her behavior, forgiveness might seem impossible. But understand that your forgiveness does not depend on the other person asking for it. It depends on you. I cannot stress that strongly enough. You cannot control what the other person does. You can only control your actions. Free yourself from your painful emotions so you can get past them. It may require some helpful support. But let me say it again that forgiveness is a major step

"Understand that your forgiveness does not depend on the other person asking for it. It depends on you."

in letting go. Learn to pry it out of your heart and loosen it from your hands. Let it go, for good.

Healing Comes in the Mourning

If you're yearning for a comfortable place right now, there may not be one immediately available. This is a hard time, but you will get through this passage, I assure you. You will pass through hurt and face new life experiences. I know this because I have lived it. After I grieved and did my initial forgiving and healing, there were wonderful experiences awaiting me. They involved hiking unknown mountains, visiting New York City, the Bahamas, and taking cruises to tropical islands. The greatest of all was to meet wonderful people from various backgrounds and cultures. There are six billion people on planet earth. Why allow one person to keep you from living and enjoying the rest of your life? To mourn is a step forward. Of course, you must be ready and willing to face what hurts so you can leave it behind and move on.

There will be days when you'd rather just pull the blankets over your head and call it quits. Be kind to yourself when you've had too much. Give yourself the necessary time to work through the process of mourning. The time varies for each of us, and it is not as fast as we wish. You may actually pull the covers over your head some days. Do it, but just be aware that this too shall pass, and there will

"There are six billion people on planet earth. Why allow one person to keep you from living and enjoying the rest of your life? To mourn is a step forward."

be better days coming. Hang onto your hope and faith. Grieving and mourning release the pain physically and emotionally.

There is so much possibility in tomorrow. If you are too down to see it right now, let me remind you that life is a wonderful gift that has only been partially opened. There is so much to experience on the other side of this. The process of healing takes time and it is not a smooth progression but a continual, at times bumpy, up and down process. It is often two steps forward and one step back. At one moment you may be feeling good, having a great time, and an hour later you may feel totally alone because you hurt so deeply and the reality of the situation has overwhelmed you.

Healing requires that you do your part. Healing requires you to act before it's comfortable and probably before you feel you're ready. It was through counseling that I learned to unleash the pain, so I could let it go. "Go" is the main action verb here. No one trains you how to grieve. If you listen carefully, your body will naturally tell you, but it is easy to squelch it, to feel that you have to be brave, a trooper, a survivor. This is especially true if there are children depending on you. Looking back, I realize that learning to allow myself to grieve was more important than I perceived at the time. Even now, ten years later, as I write these words, I grieve in a different way, but I do grieve. Thankfully, the pain is substantially diminished.

"The process of healing takes time and it is not a smooth progression but a continual, at times bumpy, up and down process. It is often two steps forward and one step back."

Three Single Thoughts to Consider

- *When have you had days when you want to pull the blankets over your head and call it quits? How did you help yourself?*
- *When you review your recent loss, what kind of progress have you made?*
- *What visions do you hold of better days and a bright future?*

"My Christian faith played a vital part in my healing. My personal faith in Jesus Christ and His intimate Holy Spirit caring for me was my mainstay during the divorce and all through my life."

My Christian faith played a vital part in my healing. My personal faith in Jesus Christ and His intimate Holy Spirit caring for me was my mainstay during the divorce and all through my life. It was vital for me to know my calamity was known by Him and I was not alone. Oddly enough, some people run away from their spirituality during painful times. In their confusion, they sometimes direct their anger or blame toward God. I know that He is not afraid of our anger or our grief. He offers to meet us in whatever state we are in. He longs to be the source of intimate care through our pain and crisis. For me, God was an intimate and a major part of the healing process.

Churches have disappointed many divorced people. Churches are made up of well intentioned humans, some of whom are misguided "religious" people, and portray not the compassion of Christ. Please understand whenever people disappoint us, or fail to live up to our expectations, it is imperative to look past people and turn toward the ultimate source of compassion and grace - Christ. Perhaps we are unrealistic in what we think the church or others can and should do. And if you lost your spouse, this time may have a dramatic withdrawal or a heightened sensitivity to the spiritual. From what I have seen, the majority of time it is the heightened experience, because it is a time when God can come the closest to your soul. Search for the depths of wisdom and comfort that can be discovered during this time. And find the church that best demonstrates what you need and are looking for.

Grieving Loss Through Death

I have three men friends, who each experienced the loss of their beloved wives. I asked them a series of questions to better understand the differences and similarities between divorce and death. In many ways loss is loss, although the specifics may be quite different. You may appreciate what my friends had to say.

Question 1 - What helped you the most to cope with the death of your wife? Each of them mentioned their children and the importance of focusing on their children's welfare. There was comfort in having children, to still be part of a family unit. All three of these men lost their wives to illness so there was time to prepare for the impending death. Each said they used the time to say their goodbyes.

Question 2 - How did you handle the quiet times alone after their death? Staying as busy as possible helped. Although busy, they still found time for introspection and realized the blessings that were in their life. One man stated that he cried often to release his emotions.

Question 3 - Was your spiritual experience or belief heightened or diminished? It was spirituality that helped one of my friends get through it. He explained that his spirituality included surprise that something like this could happen to him. He felt anger that his life partner was gone. He also felt fear of mortality and fear of the future. One man became less dogmatic than he had been in the past. The other stated that his spirituality heightened and was still growing. One friend stated, "many become angry with God and ask why me?" I asked why not me? People die everyday on this planet and with six billion of us, someone is hurting somewhere."

"Grief lessens with time, and good memories replace grief. "

Question 4 - Have you now, or will you ever stop grieving? Grief lessens with time, they responded and good memories replaced their grief. These men recognized that there's a choice, to move forward or stay stuck in the past. One of my friends talked about being thankful for life now. They all said that it takes time to process the grief. Some sad feelings may still be there, but it is different than mourning.

Question 5 - What would you suggest to those who have recently lost the love of their lives? Grieve, get angry, always talk. Listen, communicate - continue to grow and learn. Depending on time alone is not enough to get through the process. It takes work, difficult work. Be thankful for the blessings in your life, maintain perspective. We think we control what happens in our lives, but we control very little. Create a new way of looking at the world and get on with life. Focus on the positive. Don't clam up. Don't live in a shell and don't be afraid. Be open to life; live, pray, journal and exercise. One stated that exercise helped him in several ways. Running gave him time to be alone, time to think, time to talk to his deceased wife, time to talk to God; physically it was a huge stress reliever. He suggests that you let yourself vent, be angry, grieve, "get pissed off." Consider a counselor. Understand that it takes time. Give yourself the luxury of being OK with yourself, accept being alone, and then when you're ready, move on.

"Create a new way of looking at the world and get on with life. Focus on the positive. Don't clam up. Don't live in a shell and don't be afraid."

Question 8 - Who was their confidante during this time? For one, a best friend listened, and gave him honest feedback. He said that during this time, you need straight talk. You may not be thinking rationally and may need some clear, candid input. Listen to it. Listen to friends and anyone who has been widowed. It helped to know others have experienced some of the same feelings, but sometimes it's just you alone. At times, two of them talked to everyone and anyone who would listen.

Question 9 - How many years ago was your loss? How long did it take for you to make the adjustment to life alone? Overwhelmingly, my friends said that it is an ongoing adjustment, even after as long as six years. We're all different but probably it will take one or two years to begin to get comfortable with the loss. Time is not as important as the fact that you deal with it. You must get on with life. You cannot change the past. Even years later, though, doing some things around the house still seems odd. The adjustment is gradual. When the children left home, it made being alone more real. It's important to remember the positives, the good memories you had, and try not to focus too much on the loss. Make life the best it can be. Avoid negative energy. No one else will change your life, so you have to do it. Don't focus on what could have been.

My three friends also suggested that it helps to talk with people in your place of worship. Find a support group. One man made this hopeful comment. "It is a wonderful

"Time is not as important as the fact that you deal with it. You must get on with life. You cannot change the past."

thing to look forward to the rest of your life and get excited about it. You can."

Coping skills can give you immediate relief. Distractions can give you an opportunity to turn away from the intensity. Grieving is a necessary step that brings about faster healing. Healing comes in the mourning. By facing your emotions and dealing with them, you allow yourself to process the grief so you can move on. Grieving with an open heart allows forgiveness to heal further and grow into the person you are becoming. In this way, you can move on to the rest of your life.

Three Single Thoughts to Consider

- *In reading my friend's comments, which resonated with you the most?*
- *What have you done for yourself to assist in your own healing?*
- *What wisdom or insight applied to your life will help you heal and move on?*

"Grieving is a necessary step that brings about faster healing. Healing comes in the mourning."

Chapter 3

Wisdom of the Gut

"Usually when the distractions of daily life deplete our energy, the first thing we eliminate is the thing we need the most; quiet reflective time. Time to dream, time to think, time to contemplate what's working and what's not, so we can make changes for the better."

Sarah Ban Breathnach

As you start rebuilding your life, decision-making becomes a powerful force. This is a critical time for decisions and choices. There are legal decisions, property exchange decisions, new mortgages to secure, parenting issues, possession of cars, and custody and care of the kids. As you go through this time in your life, your mind may not be in the best emotional place to make these critical decisions. Regardless, if you're ready or not, decisions must be made because life doesn't stop or even slow down because of your difficult circumstances. The decisions made now, can propel you forward or take you on the slippery slope backwards. This is the time to access your inner wisdom. You'll need discernment and good judgment to make the choices that will launch your new life and keep it headed in the right direction. You'll need to sharpen your intuitive skills.

Beyond Emotions, Beyond Logical Thinking

Sound decision-making requires something beyond emotions and beyond your head. It requires wisdom within your gut. Undoubtedly, you are an intelligent person who has, and will, make many incredibly smart decisions. However, I also know that your emotions and your mind may still be in chaos from your loss and can influence you to make some unwise choices. Intelligent women and men make some not so intelligent decisions during this transition due to their emotions running amok as they become single. So, to access the best decisions, I encourage you to tap into, and trust, the wisdom of your gut at a new and deeper level.

"I consider "the gut" as the inner voice of guidance. It is the radar of your spirit that sends you messages that are definite, strong and true."

The "Gut" Defined

I consider "the gut" as the inner voice of guidance. It is part intuition, part instinct, and part wisdom. It reflects the innermost core of your being. It is the radar of your spirit that sends you messages that are definite, strong and true. You could describe the gut as a voice, or maybe an urge. Most people consider the gut more than a good guess, but less than being psychic. It signals a sense of direction you should take. It's vital you learn to pay attention to your gut so that you can make those life-changing decisions correctly.

You've heard people say, "I just had this feeling", or "Something just told me." We all periodically have that sense to some degree, but now is a perfect time to be sensitive to and depend upon your "gut", and to learn to tap into this God-given wisdom and common sense. There is good information and direction out there, nearly everywhere from those around you, but not all of it is the best for you. So, you'll need to learn to trust yourself. Trust your "gut" to tell the truth. Emotions may change, but the gut is more stable. There are times when the emotions and logic cannot be trusted. You need the direction of your gut.

"There are times when the emotions and logic cannot be trusted. You need the direction of your gut."

Neglecting the Gut Wisdom

Think about times in the past when you've refused to listen to your gut's common sense message. Later on you may have been filled with regret over your faulty decision-making. But when you've taken the time to listen to your inner wisdom, you probably enjoyed a better outcome. Of course, it's hard when things feel so out of control and so many well-intentioned friends or family members are offering advice and suggestions. Listen to what everyone has to say, and then filter those suggestions through the wisdom of the gut before you make your decision. I can't defend the authenticity of the gut scientifically, but it has been my experience that it goes beyond raw intelligence. For me it was, and is, necessary to sit and listen to the quiet truth deep within me.

"There is something within me that knows more than I know. Trusting it can only result in healing."

Author unknown

Three Single Thoughts to Consider
- *What words of advice are you receiving from others right now and how do you feel about what you're hearing?*
- *How can you encourage or allow yourself to trust the wisdom of your gut?*
- *Is there an inner feeling that seems to run counter to the traditional response that others expect?*

"That small inner voice is sometimes hard to hear because you and I are susceptible to outside influence."

If the Gut is so Right, Why isn't it Louder?

That small inner voice is sometimes hard to hear because you and I are susceptible to outside influence. We can be influenced and confused by friends, family and even authority figures. The right decisions are often not the easiest or the most convenient, yet they are most generally right for you, now and for the long term. Good decisions made with the right information won't result in regrets. Making sound decisions that will affect you, possibly for the rest of your life, must not be taken lightly, nor should it be delegated to others.

"To make the right choices in life, you have to get in touch with your soul. To do this, you need to experience solitude, which most people are afraid of, because in the silence you learn and know the solutions."   Deepak Chopra

The Process of Decision Making

In making decisions at this crucial time, it may be helpful to ask yourself the following questions, and then write out your responses. Writing down your thoughts clarifies more than merely thinking about them.

1. How will this impact me now? What effect will it have in five years or longer?
2. What is the potential for benefit, as well as the potential for loss?
3. Why do I want this? Is it realistic? Am I following my true self?
4. What is my motive for making this decision? Am I trying to prove something to myself or to someone else?
5. What else do I need to know before I make a final decision and take action?

Why Don't We Listen to Our Gut?

There are a number of reasons why we don't listen to what we know deeply within us is right. We often cave to the pressure and expectations of what others want or what we perceive they want. Perfectionism may paralyze us; we may fear making a mistake. We may immerse ourselves in so many activities, or get overwhelmed with trivial issues, so we rush to the most obvious decision instead of thinking it through. Or we may be thinking short term instead of long term.

It's important to ask probing questions to determine what will be the best decision within the context of our lives. We are often driven by duty, guilt or obligation, rather than free choice. Consequently, when we listen to the voices of those around us and not our own, we can easily rush or be pushed into a faulty decision.

"Consequently, when we listen to the voices of those around us and not our own, we can easily rush or be pushed into a faulty decision."

The Turning Point

Years ago, my sister and I were vacationing in another state. She was driving a truck and trying to make a left hand turn at a busy intersection. She was very hesitant and indecisive because she was in unfamiliar territory. She couldn't judge or predict the flow of the oncoming traffic. The guy behind us thought she was taking far too long to make the turn and shouted "Lady, just make a decision - even if it's wrong!" That may be how you feel. You know something needs to be done, but you're not sure what. Instead of freely choosing, you may feel pressured by others and obligated to act rashly.

After the trauma of the transition to singlehood subsides and you have grieved enough to begin healing, you'll naturally learn to listen to your true spirit. You'll learn to start trusting your own gut for guidance, instead of listening to the expectations of others, and feeling pressured to act. You'll be guiding your own course in life instead of being driven by others. You'll become more confident in yourself by turning toward your own spirit.

I'm suggesting you trust your inner wisdom, but that doesn't mean all of your decisions will be perfect. You may make mistakes in judgment due to your grieving or the disorienting process of becoming single. Or, perhaps you'll simply misjudge a situation. Be kind to yourself. You won't do everything right, but you can minimize bad decisions by listening to your inner voice - your gut.

Ask for Advice

The gut feeds on good advice, but often we don't ask for it. Find a safe, knowledgeable person you can be vulnerable with and start asking lots of questions for counsel and direction. The key words here are safe and knowledgeable. At this point, avoid salespeople who seek their best interest ahead of your own. Life after divorce or

"After the trauma of the transition to singlehood subsides and you have grieved enough to begin healing, you'll naturally learn to listen to your true spirit."

the death of a loved one is extremely unsettling. You no longer have a sounding board in your partner. The decision making component you once relied on is no longer there. Forget your pride. Ask, listen, and discover what works best for you. You will not live well, unless you choose well. Choose decisions that fit your situation and the outcomes you desire. Please keep in mind that the better and more specific your questions, the better and more appropriate your answers. Your gut may not have all the right answers, but it will prompt you to ask all the right questions.

Three Single Thoughts to Consider

"You will not live well, unless you choose well. "

- *Who are some knowledgeable, safe people you can ask for advice in their respected areas of expertise?*
- *In what area do you most need to seek advice right now?*
- *How much time are you spending in quiet reflection so you can listen to your own gut?*

Calculated Risk

Listen to your gut as you take risks in your life. Risks can range from choosing investment plans, purchasing a house, to buying that new sexy little black dress for the women. Once you are on your own, you'll face decisions you've never had to make before, socially, financially, professionally. Making such decisions will require some risk. After becoming single, I learned how important it was to ask questions from experts in their field. Their opinions were valuable to me then, and still helpful to this day. With proper advice, you can blend what you learn with what you know.

The Wisdom to Let Things Go

Based on my experience and the experiences of others who are newly single, you also need to make decisions about what to hold onto and what to let go of. It requires wisdom to know what's worth hanging onto. It is best if at all possible not to make any major decisions in the first year after a divorce or death of a spouse. Give yourself time to adjust, build your confidence, and clarify your thought process.

The time will come (often before you're ready) when you will face those major decisions. One decision for me, and a common one for many of us, is whether or not to keep the house. My home was an incredible place in the country, with eight acres, a large pond and woods filled with wildflowers like trillium, jack-in-the-pulpit and wildlife. I have wonderful memories of that home. We had parties for the kids and friends, camping reunions, church groups and more. I used to walk the four wooded acres several times a week. This place was more than a home, it felt like my soul lived there. I was able to watch deer wade in the creek back in the woods and it was my sanctuary.

One evening, two years after the divorce, as I had finished the four hour ritual of mowing the yard, I made a big campfire near the water. As I looked around, I realized I was alone. The kids had their own lives, and here I was. I had a decision to make. Should I keep this wonderful, yet demanding place or should I choose to have a life? I could not have both. Although I loved my homestead and all its wonderful memories, it was very time consuming and expensive to maintain. I had to look long and hard at the reality. I had to move through my emotions to the facts, beyond the past to my future. Though I felt part of my soul lived there, it was time to let it go. I had to use my head and my gut to risk breaking loose and moving on from the past to find a new future. You may find as well, that you'll have to let go of some wonderful things to make way for a future of new wonderful things. That is the nature of change. Learn to embrace change instead of resisting it.

"I had to look long and hard at the reality. I had to move through my emotions to the facts, beyond the past to my future. Anticipate a future with new joys as you tuck away the joys of the past."

Everything Has a Season

In life, there are seasons, and these seasons will bring change. You are going through one of life's biggest changes right now. Don't hold on to something past its season. You'll be able to determine what that is within your gut. It's hard to let go, so you must focus on the good that can come of the change. Anticipate a future with new joys as you tuck away the joys of the past.

As I found the time to let go of certain things and move on, you will too. The time has passed and the seasons have changed. You may, for a number of reasons, have to make immediate and drastic change in your life now. Maybe you will have no choice or limited choices, as difficult as that is, listen to your sense within your gut. Perhaps you will keep the house or other things of your past life. In time you will recognize the truth of what your gut is telling you to do.

Letting go is a skill I had to learn, not only with the house, but with the family I had married into. No longer were they my own. With the divorce, I once again became an outsider. There were surprises and disappointments, but I learned amazing lessons in human nature. Adjusting to singlehood provides you with the experience of letting go, whether you want it or not. The key is not to dwell on the past, but to see where and how things fit into your present and your future. Be true to yourself. Avoid rationalizing or justifying actions that don't serve you well. Avoid behavior and the holding onto things of the past that aren't good for you and undermine the new life you're trying to build.

"The key is not to dwell on the past, but to see where and how things fit into your present and your future. Be true to yourself."

Dethroning the Queen of Rationalization

Oh, the amazing ways we may deceive ourselves in believing things that aren't true, denying reality and trying to make what doesn't fit, fit. We want to have life the way we want it, rather than the way it is. Trying to control too much, we become the "Queen of Rationalization" (Kings included). Without self-restraint we may become really good at believing what we want in our lives, whether it's true or not. We make excuses to justify our actions. In essence, we think we have the power to create our own reality. If we don't allow the gut to do its job, we can rationalize anything;

"In essence we think we have the power to create our own reality. If we don't allow the gut to do its job, we can rationalize anything."

- My credit card can handle one more purchase; I'll pay off the credit card, next paycheck.

- That decision can wait for tomorrow; I'll deal with it later, but I'm still in control of it.

- I deserve that new car, somehow it will fit into my budget.

- I will do this because I deserve it after what I've been through.

- My child's just tired, that's why he's having this temper tantrum.

- The kids are doing fine through this divorce, they're not rebelling, therefore they must be alright.

- I'm not overeating, I'm searching comfort.

- I can afford this one extravagance because they've been talking about giving us bonuses at the end of the year.

- I don't need to talk this out, I'll handle it on my own.

- My teenager is just too emotional to deal with now.

- I'm doing good….no, really!

Not only do we rationalize our actions and thoughts, we rationalize the actions and thoughts of others too. We do this because we can't bear to see the truth or accept the reality of what is. The truth always surfaces, but not until we've wasted time rationalizing or wishing it away.

The reality of sudden singlehood can be harsh and overwhelming in many respects. Take time to retreat and reflect so you can look at things as they are. Don't rationalize that you need to give it time if you know the truth. Look at it honestly and accept it. If you deny or justify too much, you are just postponing a reality that has to be dealt with eventually. Use the "reality" test in decision-making by asking yourself to recite the facts of the situation out loud so that you can hear what "reality" you are listening to. It sounds elementary, but it can save you time and energy. Face those harsh realities as they are, look at your options, make your decision, and then you will be empowered to get on with your life. You know this, as you listen to your gut impressing upon you the right way to go – I hope you're listening!

"In all the confusion that comes in times of chaos, we search for peace. Peace is priceless."

Searching for Peace

In all the confusion that comes in times of chaos, we search for peace. Peace is priceless. Your gut is seeking peaceful options through your struggles "I want peace, give me peace," might be coming from your core. Despite all the crazy and creative ways people try to cope during tough times, they are seeking peace most of all. Listen to the choices that will bring you peace. This transition is anything but peaceful. Listen to your gut and it will reveal to you what your longings are and the peace that you search for. It will not be found in gaining and maintaining possessions, like a house, a nice car, the attention, or the controlling of other people.

Peace is not just the absence of conflict. Peace is found in quiet listening to your own gut's wisdom and making the right decisions for you. Your inner voice will direct you toward the wisest choices that will help you make sound decisions, set boundaries and seek healthy relationships. Your gut will direct you toward learning to know yourself better. It will direct you towards finding safe people in your life. Your gut, which most of all longs for peace, will teach you that peace is found in simplicity, even in our very complicated world.

"Peace is not just the absence of conflict. Peace is found in quiet listening to your own gut's wisdom and making the right decisions for you."

Your Gut Helps You Stay True to Yourself

I have been my most lonely when I am out of touch and not listening to my own voice and my own gut. I am out of sync when I act to please everyone else and I am ignoring my own gut, and my own God. Your spirituality is intimately intertwined with your gut. None of us need come alone to this crisis in our lives. The wisdom available to us through the Being of God becomes the source of internal wisdom that can guide us. I believe the wisdom of God is readily available and there for the asking. The book of Proverbs in the Bible is the book of wisdom. It states that wisdom is available to us and in fact it cries out in the streets to us.

"Wisdom shouts in the street, she lifts up her voice in the square; turn to my reproof, behold I will pour out my spirit on you; I will make my words known to you."

Pro.1:20,23

"And your ears will hear a word behind you; "this is the way, walk in it. Wherever you turn to the right or to the left."

Isaiah 30:21

"None of us need come alone to this crisis in our lives."

Three Single Thoughts to Consider
- *Can you recall a time when you listened to your gut and it was right on?*
- *Can you recall a time when you ignored what your gut had to say and you had to face the consequences?*
- *In what area of your life might you tend to stall or rationalize instead of facing the truth head on?*

Despite all the great advice you will receive, you need to make your own life decisions based on what you know is best for you. It takes some time to digest (or reject) the great advice you receive, so you can devise your own plan that works. By analyzing good information while listening to your gut, you will learn to trust yourself for all the life changing decisions that lie ahead.

Chapter 4
Taking Assessment

"The power of the question is the basis of all human progress."

Indira Gandhi

To start a journey requires that you know where you are in the first place. You need a map that says, "You are here." Facing a divorce or death of a loved one, you may feel disoriented, abandoned and lost. Discovering where you are now requires careful assessment. Your head may spin with questions, choices and self-doubt. You may ask yourself a thousand questions:

- Where do I go from here?

- What happens next?

- How do I pick up the pieces when my life is in shambles?

- Where do I begin?

This is the time to take an inventory of your life and your beliefs. This chapter will assist you in determining where you are right now in your beliefs, thoughts, fears, hopes, and dreams. Once these are determined, you can begin putting the pieces of your life back together and turn in a new direction. Like the mapping programs on your computer, you can zoom out and see where you want to go. Be honest in your assessment. Taking this personal inventory will require some courage. Don't overlook the difficult questions or slide through the process. This pivotal period will impact not only the next few years, but the rest of your life. What you do today, and the choices you make today, matter greatly. Now is the time to take a look at yourself in a new light. Be open, honest, and receptive. Take the steps toward discovering your new and authentic self.

"This is the time to take an inventory of your life and your beliefs."

Personal Inventory

Taking personal inventory is determining where you are now, what you have and the beliefs you hold today. For example, how are you viewing and reacting to your world? Are you angry, cautious, afraid, highly guarded? Have you become determined to never, ever again allow yourself to be vulnerable? If this is where you are today, this is a natural response to feeling hurt, abandoned, uncertain or betrayed. In facing the loss of your mate, self-protective feelings, and being guarded may surface. As you face your life alone this is understandable, but remember also, that the pain you feel right now is a temporary state; these feelings will subside and change.

I once told a man I was dating that I would never again allow myself to be as vulnerable as I once was in my marriage. I believed that I had been hurt because I was vulnerable, and as my defense I pledged that I would never again be so open. I figured this way I could avoid future pain. It's no surprise that the relationship didn't last, since a healthy mutual bond requires vulnerability on both sides. That was where I stood in the early years after my divorce. It was for a time until I worked through my healing and felt safe again. And for you now, it may not be a good idea to be too vulnerable. Through grieving and healing, you will become healthy and whole again. You'll relax your self-protections and open up again. You'll be able to determine when it is time to become open for a relationship and vulnerable again in a healthy, loving way. There's a time when you'll be able to drop the defensive, protective barriers that you naturally use during a crisis. Evaluate where you are so you can start determining where you want to go. In this chapter we will do this by using powerful questions.

"Evaluate where you are so you can start determining where you want to go."

Take your time on these questions and write them down so you can better visualize them. Generally, the first answer that comes to mind will probably be the most honest. Trust your gut.

- Is this a good, undistracted time for you to be honest with yourself?

- Are you willing to honestly assess both your strengths and weaknesses?

- Is there a subject that you are not ready to deal with right now?

- What still hurts inside of you?

- How willing are you to disclose the truth of what you're going through into words, whether written or spoken?

- How willing are you to put forth the effort to help yourself right now?

"What still hurts inside of you?"

- To what extent do you allow others to know your feelings?

- In what ways might you be sabotaging yourself right now instead of helping yourself?

- How are you encouraging yourself when you have a moment of self-doubt?

- What are the positive decisions and actions you made through this crisis in your life?

- When you think about your future, what kinds of thoughts or visions come to mind?

- What might be the outcome if you stay who you are today and where you are now?

- What attitudes and positive thoughts are helping you

handle your transition?

- What attitudes might be preventing you from fully healing or moving on?
- Are you beginning to be comfortable alone so you can enjoy or appreciate your own company?
- Are you becoming more dependent upon yourself than other people?
- What important parts of you (trust, confidence, the dreamer, adventurer, creative thinker), have suffered from this event in your life? Do you foresee yourself sometime in the near future ready to work on these again?
- Have you given up on your dreams? If so, how can you regain them?

Asking yourself these kinds of questions can give you an idea about where you are in this process. Pay attention to your responses. Feel free to create your own questions too. Ask yourself questions that you might ask a friend going through these circumstances to help them vocalize what's in their heart and mind. Ask yourself how you are handling life right now. Talk to yourself and out loud if you need to and write down your responses to help you clarify. The intensity of your current feelings will one day subside, but now your thoughts need to be brought forward. The thoughts and feelings that seem so

"Are you beginning to be comfortable alone so you can enjoy or appreciate your own company?"

pronounced right now will subside as you bring them forth to examine them and through their examining them you can slowly start regaining your balance.

During Our Lifetime, We are Different People

If you were to define who you were ten years ago, this description may have little resemblance to who you are now or where you find yourself today. Your past can be used as a guidepost of where you've been and a starting point to begin your future. That's the purpose here, to see where you are and begin planning the steps that will transport you toward the next era in your life.

An Honest Look

Exposing your inner thoughts, feelings, and perceptions helps you better deal with them. You gain an understanding of where you stand in your life map to begin clarifying where you can possibly go. Be straightforward and avoid defensive excuses, justifications and rationalizations. Face yourself as squarely and freely as you can, using the questions listed in this chapter as a tool to see what lies within. This will also help you decide what you want to leave behind and what to take into the future. Granted, some of your admissions might be hard to face. But there is no critical authority leaning over your shoulder to judge you. Shed your defenses and lay yourself out naked. Take a long hard look at where you are. Explore the hidden parts of your being that were forced into hiding by expectations, guilt, fear or shame. Now is a golden opportunity to rediscover dormant dreams and buried passions that seemed previously impractical or impossible. Someday soon you'll be ready to pursue them once again.

Pursuing the Answers

The questions posed in this chapter will help you to unveil your innermost thoughts and secrets. No one has to see your answers, just you. If you skim over or fail to truly consider the questions, you'll miss out. I am the first to admit that being honest with yourself can be hard work. Some of us spend entire lifetimes trying to avoid, or cover up certain issues within our thoughts and secrets. As Dr. Harold Bloomfield says, "What we resist, persists". The issues we avoid will surface in many ways and haunt us until they are dealt with. This chapter is about dealing with them. That's why I began the chapter with the list of direct questions, and there are more to come.

There is incredible power in asking good questions, the kind that trigger an understanding of where you are now and how much potential you have. The greatest teachers of self-understanding are you and the spirit of God. Truly knowing yourself comes through posing the right questions. Be open to asking yourself probing questions right now.

"I am the first to admit that being honest with yourself can be hard work. Some of us spend entire lifetimes trying to avoid, or cover up certain issues within our thoughts and secrets."

You may not have all the answers yet, but don't worry, they are there within you or yet to be found by you. I have found that some answers take time to surface, often when you're more able to deal with them. But now is the time to start exploring.

Going Inward

Find a quiet place where you can be with your thoughts, your favorite nature spot, or the room in your own house where you feel most comfortable. Be open to the first answer that comes to you at a gut level. If you come across a particularly painful point, maybe it's necessary for now to temporarily set it aside, and revisit it at a later time. Realize that once you admit to and face your major fears, insecurities or conflicts, you can in fact, render them powerless.

"Realize that once you admit to and face your major fears, insecurities or conflicts, you can in fact, render them powerless."

Taking Notes

Expressing your thoughts on paper helps discover what you are truly thinking. Writing down your thoughts and feelings, allows you to connect with your inner wisdom. For this exercise, write in your journal or even within this book. Don't analyze too deeply now (save that for later), now is the time to bring them to the forefront in admitting them. Once you allow your inner thoughts to come out and be recorded, you can revisit them later. Maybe you'll even add some notes at a later date. The purpose here is to get in touch with what is in your heart.

Facing Fears

- What are your biggest fears right now?
- What are the realistic chances of these fears coming true?
- What strength do you have within you that can handle these fears?
- In what way might they be affecting you or influencing your behavior?
- What specific things, people or activities calm your fears and bring you peace of mind?
- How can you start to use these things, people and activities for inner peace and safety to quell your fears?

"Writing down your thoughts and feelings, allows you to connect with your inner wisdom. "

Getting Clear

- What do you need or want right now, more than anything?
- Is this within the realm of possibility?
- If it is possible, how can you help yourself begin to get what you truly want?
- If it is not possible, how can you help yourself accept this?
- What is getting in the way of finding what you want or need?

Defining Your Success

- What is your personal definition of success?

- Who is the one person that you admire and consider a success?

- To what extent (or in what specific area) do you consider yourself a successful person?

- What are your strongest assets and your greatest talents?

- In what areas do you hold untapped potential?

Projecting Your Future

"What is your personal definition of success?"

- How do you envision your future?

- Write down the one definite in your life; one belief that will never change and is foundational to who you are.

- What was your dream when you graduated from high school or college?

- What is your heart's deepest desire? What do you truly long to occur in your life?

- How do you envision your ideal future, what words come to mind?

- What are the first steps you need to take so you can reorder your life to start your future? Are you beginning those steps now?

Breaking through the Blocks

- Are you aware of inner blocks or barriers of denial which impede your ability to accept or resolve what you're feeling?

- Are you still struggling with unresolved anger or emotions or do you feel you've resolved them?

- If you are angry, precisely with whom are you angry and how are you expressing this anger?

- Do angry moments appear unexpectedly?

- What is keeping you from accepting and resolving your anger?

Knowing Your Strengths

Are you fully using your personal strengths and assets right now? Knowing your strengths and weak areas can help you rally your inner resources so you can pick yourself up and move on. Several questionnaires or instruments can assist you in discovering your strengths. Two examples are DiSC and Meyers Briggs. There are numerous other self-directed instruments that show your temperament and inner strengths. These surveys are worth the time and can help you identify which of your attributes can help you become more successful and which traits can get in your way. For myself, I would have never realized my aversion to confrontation had I not been through some of these personal assessments. Identifying that, I can work to control, minimize or remove what is prevalent in my life that does not help me live fully. But first I must be conscious of them.

Working the Plan

I encourage you to look back over your answers to the questions presented in this chapter. What do they reveal about you? Are there any answers that surprised you? Note which areas require more focus or deeper understanding. Is there an area that you want to start working on now? Perhaps you've found an area that brings to the surface your potential and hope for your future.

"Your first step toward positive change doesn't have to be drastic."

As I stated earlier in this book, seeing where you are now will help you move toward where you want to go. Your first step toward positive change doesn't have to be drastic. Your first step might actually be to rest, reflect and relax for a short time so you can rebuild. Don't underestimate the power of rest and reflection in meditation and prayer. Focus on reading self-help books and finding information from healthy sources. After taking assessment, a time will come to get going and sign up, enroll, inquire, venture out, buy a ticket, and start your engine. Through personal understanding you can be guided to initiate action. Understanding will help create opportunity to step in the direction you want to head. It's your call. Which way will take you to your definition of success?

Taking on Your Heart's Desire

"The tragedy of life is not in the fact of death, but in what dies inside us while we live."   Norman Cousins

Depending on how fresh your loss is, or how deeply you feel about the lost dreams of your life, the thought of mentioning dreams of the future may sound silly or impossible to fathom. You may think, "How can I even think about my life's dreams, I've lost my greatest dream with my mate. I'm barely getting through this awful time!" The time will come where taking an in depth self-assessment will show you how to step forward to your new life and find peace of mind and life balance. Take the time to identify your personal dreams and hold onto them. They will give you hope. Your talents and gifts are sent from God to fill your life with joy, to give you balance, to help you serve others. Reacquaint yourself with your dreams by redefining them, so that when the dust settles you can begin to pursue them once again. Finding and using your talents and pursuing your dreams comprise the core of your fulfillment. No doubt, they are a large part of how you define success.

"Finding and using your talents and pursuing your dreams comprise the core of your fulfillment. No doubt, they are a large part of how you define success."

Finding the Perfect Mate or the Perfect Me?

If your heart's desire is in finding another mate,

I ask you to evaluate this notion carefully, just as you are assessing other parts of your life. A relationship or a marriage is not the answer or solution to everything. It's not the end all to your happiness. It would be well for you to contemplate if a new mate is truly the answer for you now or in the near future. Society portrays relationships as romantic "completion". It's as if each one of us are two halves waiting to become a whole. But a real relationship requires two whole people coming together, making a third dimension. The ultimate of singlehood is in becoming whole alone. In other words, wholeness comes in discovering who we are in God's beautiful design, which may or may not include another lifetime partner.

"Are you searching for the perfect mate or are you searching for the perfect self, and peace within that self? The ultimate of singlehood is in becoming whole alone."

Are you searching for the perfect mate or are you searching for the perfect self, and peace within that self? Only you can answer this question. Have you fallen prey to the over romanticizing version of what a relationship is supposed to be? Do you have a realistic and objective view of what a relationship really is? Can your loneliness be filled in other ways instead of being obsessed with finding a mate as the solution to your happiness? Are you tired of me asking so many direct questions?

Singlehood Starts With a Single Step

During your period of transition you will need to be more proactive than ever before because you are fully and completely in charge of your life. Focus on the inventory of where you are now and what you have going for you. Take note of all of the good in your life right now, despite your circumstances. Find your attitude of gratitude for what is, and then the areas you want to see change. Don't overhaul everything at once or take on the major changes too fast. Find those small areas in which you want to make slight changes that will eventually create big results in your life. Discover your potential by stepping out; and taking one single step. Be open to the opportunities of trying new things and learning from other people. Once you've assessed where you are, start devising a plan with a single step that will turn you toward the direction you want to go.

After completing this chapter, dare yourself to do something you have never done before. The discoveries you'll make about yourself, others and the world, can be exciting. Go out for lunch alone to a nice restaurant, take in a movie on your own. Go to a concert or attend an art fair in town. Find a new place that brings you peace and claim it as your sanctuary. Look at your world in a new light to enjoy those surroundings. Pursue singleness. Get in touch with yourself; start to perceive the world as an individual. Take a deep breath, stretch your horizons and take it all in as you do so.

"To dare to live alone is the rarest courage; since there are many who had rather meet their bitterest enemy in the field, than their own hearts in a closet." Charles Caleb Colton

"After completing this chapter, dare yourself to do something you have never done before. Pursue singleness."

In pursuing your new life, hopefully you will gravitate toward what you personally consider success. Is your success defined as family, status, wealth, peace of mind or charisma with people? Is it spirituality, a closeness with God; or rewarding relationships? Once you define success for yourself, it is yours to make in your new life.

Define for Me a Successful Woman

"Define for me the successful woman for she knows: If she gains the whole world and loses her children, she has nothing. If she sells her integrity, she has lost everything. Her word will stand on its own because she is honesty. People trust in her as a guidepost, a lighthouse, an anchor in the storm. She can lead a corporation and she can lead small children.

"Once you define success for yourself, it is yours to make in your new life."

She has the spirit of vision and hope to rise to the heavens, and the heart of kindness and compassion to bend to save a soul from hell. She is a mother, or she is barren of womb, she is rich, or she is poor. Life does not define her by its circumstances. She has defined life by how she reacts to it and it is good.

Through her vision for life she has set her own course. Through her wisdom, she aligns it with the way the Heavens blow the wind. If you ask the successful woman what is she all about, she will say I am about relationships, the making, the mending, the enriching of relationships. For in the end nothing else matters. She knows success is found within successful relationships.

Define for me a successful woman. She knows that life is short and the needs are many. She inspires success in the world. Her hands are strong. She takes care of her aging mother and considers it her privilege. Her spirit has the strength of steel. Yet in the wee hours of the night, she can lay her head upon the lap of God and cry when she needs to. In truth, the successful woman writes her own definition of success. For no one will tell her what she is. God knows, and she knows. And that is enough for her. The successful woman is a powerful influence. She knows and she lives that definition every day of her life."

Kathey Batey

Chapter 5

Going Solo in a World Designed for Two

"To risk is to jump into the arms of faith laughing."

You are Not One Half of Anything, You are Whole.

According to a recent U.S. Census Bureau report, the population of unmarried women will soon surpass the number of married women. The same report states that after ten years of being single, 79% of those women will remarry. That leaves a portion of women who will not. If you are a single woman, you are in good company. I realize that may not help the feeling of isolation you feel right now, but it does help to have a sense of what's realistic. It is unknown whether you need to brace yourself for extended singlehood or not, so I say prepare for living single. I also say prepare yourself for what can be a wonderful full life.

Being newly unmarried can be awkward in our society, since we are in some ways defined by our relationships. This is not only a cultural definition but for many of us what we believe is true. We are used to

"It is unknown whether you need to brace yourself for extended singlehood or not, so I say prepare for living single. I also say prepare yourself for what can be a wonderful full life."

identifying ourselves as part of a couple, and once this definition no longer applies we grapple with the missing part of our identity. This new, ambiguous status may bring back the kinds of self-conscious emotions you experienced during those insecure teen years, where you were sensitive on how you were being perceived by others.

Missing the Other Half

In the beginning of your new singlehood it may vaguely feel as if you are missing half of yourself. That's simply part of the transition you're going through. In your past, you enjoyed the comfort of having a partner nearby - of having someone else to rely on when you were in need. If you faced an important decision, you always had a sounding board. You had a place where you belonged, and it was beside someone. Even if the relationship wasn't perfect, there was a sense of value in being connected to that person, of being a vital part of their life. These images stand in stark contrast to where you are now. In the midst of many changes, you now have to be the one to double check everything. You alone make the decisions. This transition is accompanied by pain and uncertainty which makes your singleness feel foreign and awkward. It feels unnatural, like walking with one leg instead of two. Then there are the holidays, Valentines day, and New Year's Eve celebrations and other social events can be torturous reminders that you are alone. But I promise you, in time, the intensity will lessen and you will find your own stride again, on your own.

Seeing the Wholeness of the "Perfect" Couples

In being alone, you may notice those "perfect" couples that seem to make a mockery of you, the ones who seem to live the life you wanted. Don't let these perfect couples intimidate you. Acknowledge their beauty, in fact, rejoice in their beauty. You are not any less valuable or credible in their presence. The world has ample room for couples and for you too, as a single person. Reconsider and redesign the attitude that believes the world was created for couples. You and I are not less of a person because we're without a partner. Focus on the beauty of relationships, not your loss. Don't shut out opportunities in life simply because you are alone. You are not one half of anything. Believe that you are indeed a whole person. Accept, cultivate and eventually celebrate your individual uniqueness and wholeness.

"Reconsider and redesign the attitude that believes the world was created for couples. Don't shut out opportunities in life simply because you are alone."

Embrace Your Wholeness

In realizing that you are not one half, but a whole being, I want to remind you that today, at this moment, being single does not make you flawed or incomplete. In fact, you are undoubtedly in many people's eyes the idea of a perfect potential mate, exactly as you are. You just don't know that person yet, and who knows when or where life's path will take you to possibly welcome that individual into your life.

Accept who you are as the unique, exceptional person that you are. Don't allow yourself to be overcome with self-punishing thoughts…

- Why did this happen to me?
- What's wrong with me?
- Why do I have to be alone?
- How could I have taken so much for granted?"

Your Uniqueness Makes You Whole

Divorce causes needless self-doubts and insecurities to surface. Despite what changes we've experienced, you and I are still the same person deep inside, even if right now we don't have someone to appreciate it. We don't always have to have someone tell us our value. We can know it from another source: the Word of God, the scriptures, the voice of our faith. God's love defines us as highly valuable, precious and worthy of love. What better starting place could there be?

So, to answer the question, if a tree falls in the forest and no one is there to hear it, does it still make a sound? Yes it does. It is still a tree and the sound it makes has nothing to do with the fact that a person didn't show up to hear it! I encourage you to stand tall and proud and worthy of attention in the midst of others. You stand out because you are unique; because you are you, not because you stand-alone. Celebrate your uniqueness, because you are truly, wonderfully unique. No one now, or ever, will be exactly like you, anywhere. Celebrate that truth. Own it.

Redesigning Relationships

Major changes may occur in friendships when your relationship ends by divorce or by death. They might not be able to fit you into the neat package that you were before. This is not your issue, it's theirs. Be prepared that some of the friends you had when you were part of a couple may be lost during your transition into single life. This happens. Some of your relationships with couples that were once intimate may become shallow or distant. Some people just don't know how to deal with odd numbers. They are a couple, they may think in couples. Be comforted in knowing that new relationships await you. In time, you will establish new long lasting relationships as life moves forward and you step out into your new world.

Whether you have gone through divorce, or tremendous loss, you will witness some of your beliefs and views about yourself changing and shifting. As you heal, you will discover that some of your beliefs were incorrect. An aha moment may come to you if you were

"Be prepared that some of the friends you had when you were part of a couple may be lost during your transition into single life. Be comforted in knowing that new relationships await you."

in a condemning relationship and subjected to negative comments about physical features, intelligence or how you did things. Abusive relationships take their toll, but the human spirit is amazingly resilient. If you were exposed to abuse, criticism and rejection, you may have begun to doubt yourself. But once alone, you can discover that these negative things were not true about you at all. That will be a liberating moment for you.

We Act On What We Believe

We all have our own odd rules and expectations about how people are supposed to act, and how we are suppose to act. We have ideas about what we can or cannot do, like thinking we aren't suppose to go to an event or restaurant alone, or that the world is made for couples and if we're not part of a couple we just don't fit in. Where do these ideas come from? It's probably a combination of personal and cultural expectations. I now understand that the world is not designed for couples only. They are not the only ones with fulfilled and happy lives; many single people are. I encourage you to quit worrying about what people think or expect from you. Create your own ideas of how you want to behave. Don't let those expectations or odd rules that you or others have stop you from venturing into your new life. Listen to what your heart really wants

"Abusive relationships take their toll, but the human spirit is amazingly resilient."

to do and then do it. Reconsider and re-evaluate what you do based on the way it's always been.

Finding Your Value

Where does your sense of value come from? Many of us feel valued through the life roles we fill (wife, mother, daughter, sister, friend, professional title, etc.) Can you define who you are without using roles? For many of us this is difficult, because much of how we define ourselves is connected to our roles. A life transition requires redefining who you are and where your value comes from. It helps to clarify (or rediscover) what defines you and gives you power in your life. My point is, if you can redefine your value, you can change your perspective. Your outlook will change and shift as you clarify your self-identity and you progress through this transition.

The old life won't fit anymore. Things will be different. You'll be different. Don't despair at that thought. Instead, be intrigued by it and start to see the possibilities. It's a perfect time to redesign your world.

"I now understand that the world is not designed for couples only. They are not the only ones with fulfilled and happy lives; many single people are."

Four Single Thoughts to Consider
- *What words would you use to define yourself without using social roles?*
- *Can you explain in detail the definitions or descriptions you stated, for example, if you're creative, describe in detail how*

are you creative?

- *In the past, what activity did you believe could only be done as a couple and why?*
- *What is the most important way you have defined or redefined your value?*

Redesigning Your World

You start redesigning your world by changing your mindset. We tend to live our lives based on what we believe, whether we're right or not. You, like everyone else, have essentially created your personal perception of the world in which you live and how things are supposed to be. Now is a great time to redesign your world and how you view it. In your new beginning, you get to determine who you are and how fully you will participate in your own life.

"You have to be the first to believe that being single can mean being strong."

You may need to change your mindset first. It may take some effort to shift your thinking. You have to be the first to believe that being single can mean being strong. Being alone is a circumstance that anyone can find themselves in. Believe you are whole and capable and start to act like it. You have past successes – independent acts that helped define you. Don't discount their importance or gloss them over. I encourage you to make a list of your past successes and accomplishments - perhaps you've forgotten many of them.

What are you most proud of? Reconsider the skills

and strengths you possess, especially the ones that have been disregarded or underestimated in the past.

Remember those dreams you once had? Now is the time to revive them, to haul them out of the attic of your mind and review them. Take this opportunity to be strong on your own and redefine who you are in the world. This is the time to focus on yourself. Perhaps it's been a long time since you've done this. Now is the time to be redesigning your world. Redesign it from the inside out. Redecorate your own soul first. Bring all of your major assets and skills to the forefront to create a more balanced picture of where you are now, and how much potential you have.

Set up a Personal Network

As you redesign your world, it is vital to build and maintain professional and personal relationships. This is your network. If you already have some solid relationships to strengthen, honor them now. Reinforce the bonds you share with others. Value your dearest friends and family members. Don't avoid certain friends due to your current state. Seek them out and let them know you're still available, alive and ready to move on with your new life. Invite others out for lunch, make quick phone calls or write some notes.

Stay as positive as possible and focus on strengthening your network of relationships. Appreciate

"Stay as positive as possible and focus on strengthening your network of relationships."

those who will help you maintain your physical world. Pay them well. So if the pipes break in the middle of the night, you can call upon your maintenance technicians and not feel guilty. You will feel like a stronger person, more worthwhile if you show appreciation to others with tips or honest wages. If money is an issue, find other ways to compensate by babysitting, errands, or special favors. Be creative. Issues like broken pipes will force you to reach out and build that network, whether you want to or not. It is much easier to have them established before trouble comes and having them established gives you peace of mind.

"You may resist the idea of enlarging your personal network, thinking it wouldn't be comfortable right now. You're already out of your comfort zone anyway, so why not?"

You may resist the idea of enlarging your personal network, thinking it wouldn't be comfortable right now. You're already out of your comfort zone anyway, so why not? Get curious about new activities and social circles, begin to explore the world around you. Open your mind to new ideas, and watch for opportunities to learn, to grow, and expand your world. Introduce yourself to a new social climate. Join a gym, get involved in a book club or discussion group. Volunteer. Take a dance class or find an area of study. Learn a new skill. Broaden your horizons so you can intelligently converse on social issues, literature, art, or other pursuits. The possibilities are endless, just like your world is. Don't be afraid to fail at a new venture, fear will paralyze you if you allow it. Build that network to build your new life.

Branching Out

It may be natural during a time of transition and loss to feel that you want to withdraw or hide from the world. This is understandable but it isn't healthy to withdraw for an extended length of time. By withdrawing, you may feel you are controlling your environment and truly keeping things safe, but you are also missing out on opportunities for growth, adventure and good things to come. We all need to belong, especially during tough times. This is a basic human need. And yet, you may be tempted to shut out the world, to shield yourself from more hurt. I understand, but I encourage you to do the exact opposite. Instead of wrapping up in self-protection, open up instead.

In times of crisis, our world comes to a screeching halt while everyone else keeps moving along. You may wonder, how can people possibly continue to get wrapped up in mundane issues like TV shows, gossip, fashion, schedules, sports or activities while your heart is being torn from your chest. The world does go on, regardless. You may look around and see people smiling, laughing and living their lives. It is time to make the decision for one of those vibrant people to be you.

"You may be tempted to shut out the world, to shield yourself from more hurt. I understand, but I encourage you to do the exact opposite. Instead of wrapping up in self-protection, open up instead."

Four Single Thoughts to Consider

- *Have you been tempted to withdraw from people and how have you handled the urge?*

- *Who is in your personal network? List them. Who would you call in the middle of the night if the car breaks down, or if you locked yourself out of the house?*
- *Whose social network list are you on and what can you do for that person?*
- *What activity or social area could you get involved in, so you can expand your world?*

Redesigning Your Journey

The first step in redesigning your journey is determining where you really want to go. Do you want to go back to school, change careers, start a career, attend the theatre, go to a festival, the beach, a tourist town, or take a trip? What is stopping you? Are you telling yourself it's easier to stay home? Do you insist that the kids need you and therefore anything you want and need isn't valid? They do need you tremendously, but this can also be used as an excuse to avoid your own life. No money? Visit a bookstore, attend lectures, walk the lakeshore, go to a park, visit an art gallery, go to the museum. Take note of when you are making excuses, and then direct yourself into doing what could turn out to be a delightful surprise.

At first, it is easy to make excuses to keep yourself from branching out, but I hope you will catch yourself and decide you've had enough hiding. I hope you will get to the healing point and realize that you have to step out to live

"The first step in redesigning your journey is determining where you really want to go."

your life! Realize that your life is up to you and you will never find adventure or growth by watching other people do their thing and live their lives. Don't escape life, find it. Turn toward life and its opportunities and try new things to embrace and redesign your life.

Don't sit and watch people living pretend lives on the television set. Make your own movie of life - you have the starring role! This is your second act and it can be the best part. Remember what you dreamed of long ago, before you were overcome with everyday life and struggles or relationship problems? Do you even remember what you truly wanted for your life? What got in the way? I know the world may look dark and scary sometimes, but don't let discomfort stop you. Maybe you're just seeing the shadow side of something wonderful - something that can help you develop, grow and reach out. Seek those new experiences. Opportunities await you that will help you grow and flourish. Find them.

"Don't escape life, find it. Opportunities await you that will help you grow and flourish. Find them."

Finding Courage for the Journey

Courage is being afraid and doing it anyway. It is the result of freeing yourself from blocks and barriers. Don't let yourself be intimidated by fear. Find safe places, step out and stretch yourself. Yes, it's sometimes easier to stay home and stay in the small confines of your present life, thinking this is all life is – surviving. Yes, you will have moments of feeling awkward, afraid or insecure. You may find yourself with tears in your eyes or a lump in your throat. Step out anyway. That's why we have tissues. Strengthening your comfort zone can be stressful. It feels easier to stay home in your sweats and be alone. By protecting yourself from the possibility of getting hurt, you end up missing out. Don't settle for a life that consists of routines.

When you force yourself to step out of your comfort zone you may be relieved when it's over. Commend yourself. Congratulate yourself for the courage it took to venture out to uncharted territory and scary experiences. Just do it. Even if things don't end up perfectly, give yourself credit for having the gumption to try. Every journey begins with a single step.

"You give yourself a tremendous gift when you learn to enjoy your own company. Pursue singleness; pursue you! "

Party of One

You give yourself a tremendous gift when you learn to enjoy your own company. Pursue singleness; pursue you! The evening will come when you have nothing planned, but you don't feel like staying home. What will you do with this time? Will you simply flip on the TV and watch reruns or will you take yourself out on a date? Bookstores are a great place to start. Especially the ones that have coffee or pastry bars. Let yourself hang out and browse a few books. Bookstores offer a quiet, safe and relaxed environment.

Find a friendly coffee shop that suits you. Take

yourself to a favorite restaurant with an outside eating area, a garden room or one overlooking the water, if you're so lucky to have such a place near you. Discover charming little towns that intrigue you. Visit unique shops and take your journal. Find a nearby park or café and take in your surroundings. This is your life. Take it all in with deep breaths and appreciation for who you are and who you are becoming. Don't simply react to life. Make it happen.

Be Stronger Than Your Emotions

At any time, at any unguarded moment, during the early stages of your transition you can get swept away by emotions. This may sound odd, but there will be times when you must simply plow through or step over what you're feeling. Be realistic. Look at the big picture. Of all the billions of people on this earth, if one doesn't want your company, others will. As you heal, you'll be able to override self-doubt and other negative feelings. My suggestion is not to wait until you feel ready, but challenge yourself to do it now. Those insecure feelings may just disappear through the front door the next time you step out of it. There are too many experiences awaiting you. There are cultures to explore, hobbies to take up, people to meet, places to go, dance floors to dance on, fascinating conversations to be had and people to learn from. There are also individuals who need to learn from you, to benefit from you. Your

"This is your life. Take it all in with deep breaths and appreciation for who you are and who you are becoming. Don't simply react to life. Make it happen."

loss does not define you. Take on your world. Start within your own community. If you have available time, search for volunteer opportunities, venture into new clubs or join a support group. Mingle, get acquainted, actively rebuild your life and cultivate new interests. Watch for the opportunity and step toward it. If you have children, you can certainly make many of these suggestions as family time, but find those "alone" moments for yourself as well.

There Will Be Lonely Times

"I realized no matter how lonely this moment was, it was not nearly as lonely as I was when I was married. No isolation is like praying for a connection with your partner who is emotionally absent."

There will be times when there is no upbeat advice, no distraction or diversion will give you the comfort you need. Loneliness can crowd in and engulf you like a dark, thick fog so you can no longer see the joy and adventure in your world. This is the time to redesign your thinking. I remember one particularly lonely spring night. I was walking through an outdoor gardening area at a local flower shop. It was a chilly spring day and no one was in the garden area but me. Shopping for flowers is usually one of my favorite, brightest times, but at that moment, I was overcome with loneliness. There was no one to share the new flowers of spring with me. The isolation was suffocating, literally, figuratively and even spiritually. I even felt a bit afraid. As I stood in that flower shop, a powerful insight came to me, a beautiful moment of truth. I realized no matter how lonely this moment was, it was not nearly as lonely as I was when I was married. Since that moment, I've heard others say the same truth, that while there are moments of loneliness when you're on your own, there is nothing so lonely as being with someone and being lonely. No isolation is like praying for a connection with your partner who is emotionally absent.

I felt better, suddenly the flowers looked brighter and the self-pity stopped. I was comforted by the knowledge that being alone and on my own was indeed better than being lonely with someone. The pity I felt then was for those I have known (myself included), who spent many lonely hours, days and years in an impossible relationship. I bought myself some flowers that day, a lot of flowers, in fact, a huge bouquet. I learned the simple comfort in taking a deep breath and finding the truth in that transformational moment. I hope you will find your own moment of truth. And then, buy yourself some flowers.

"I was comforted by the knowledge that being alone and on my own was indeed better than being lonely with someone."

Redesigning You

"To be nobody but yourself in a world which is doing its best night and day to make you everybody else means to fight the hardest battle which any human being can fight and never stop fighting."

ee cummings

Who's Talking to You?

Throughout our life, our thoughts direct us in all that we do. It is our attitude and perceptions that drive us to try and succeed or never to try at all. Be mindful of how you talk to yourself – how you encourage or discourage yourself. Self-talk will either get you through this crisis or stop you in your tracks. Don't allow negative self-talk to let you miss out on your party of life. Ninety five percent of a successful life is simply showing up!

Below is a comparison of the self-talk that may go on in your head when we go out alone and feel like you're an odd ball or the square peg in the round hole.

"Self-talk will either get you through this crisis or stop you in your tracks."

Your thoughts when you are out alone:	Others' thoughts when you are out alone
I look ridiculous	A decent woman alone
There are only couples here!	A single woman alone
I can't stand being out alone!	Woman alone
I won't survive this, I'm suffocating!	Woman alone, looking around
No one here talk to	Woman alone, looking down at the floor

In comparing your personal self-talk to what others might be thinking, consider this, your own self-talk is full of emotion, while other people's thoughts are objective. Try to keep your self-talk neutral and objective. Don't panic. Consider this self-talk instead: I am here, I am alone, and I refuse to be self-conscious. I will step out of my ego and insecurities and move forward. As you look around say to yourself, I will take everything in so I can enjoy myself. Appreciate the moment, be in the present. Don't focus on being alone, focus on what's happening in the world that surrounds you. Just live your life. Chances are very good that those around you are too caught up in their own situation to dwell on yours.

Finding Interesting Faces

If you find, (like I did) that you yearn for more interesting people and events in your life, then you need to be open in the company of interesting people. Maybe you're wondering how to do that. It begins with exposing yourself to places where interesting people hang out. As I mention earlier in this book, the theatre, bookstores, nice restaurants, lectures, art galleries, libraries or night courses might be a good start. Reach out of your comfort zone and take the risk to be around different people. Make a true effort to meet and learn from others. If you are a student of human interaction, like I am, watch how people interact and see what you can learn from them. You will find that other people's experiences will encourage you to create

"Don't focus on being alone, focus on what's happening in the world that surrounds you. Just live your life."

your own interesting experiences. Observe and listen more than you speak.

The Art of Conversation

If you want to truly redesign yourself, being aware of your communication skills is a great place to start. How you communicate reveals a lot about you, and it is a skill that can be improved. Good conversation skills are an art, and just like the art of singing and painting, few of us are really good at it; we all have different skill levels. Start paying more attention to your conversations. Even when you're in the midst of grieving and still hurting, listening to another person's troubles instead of talking about your own can be a respite. Ask questions to further the discussion. Hold back on revealing your own story until the other person's story is complete. Focus on the other person. When you do speak, ask questions that go deeper than surface conversations, such as weather, work, or gossip. Look for interesting subjects such as current events, literature and philosophy. Reach past the mundane and excessive details that really add nothing to the conversation. Find something stimulating to discuss that adds value and growth to your life and the person you are speaking with.

"How you communicate reveals a lot about you, and it is a skill that can be improved."

Redesign Your Listening Skills

Just as you redesign yourself, you can redesign

your conversation skills. Truth be told, there are very few good listeners in our world. When you find them, they are precious. Good listeners nurture your soul. They ask a lot of questions because they truly want to hear what other people are thinking. They search for depth. If you want to get to the core of who a person truly is, you have to listen. Good listening is paying attention to the things that aren't necessarily being said. It's making an authentic connection with another human being. It's accepting who they are without judgment or condition. Listen to your next conversation and ask yourself if you sound like someone you would like to be around or considered good company.

Seven Single Thoughts to Consider

- *Do you use "I" constantly in your conversations?*
- *Do you discuss important issues or only the ordinary, the details, or the mundane?*
- *Do you really listen to the person or do all the talking?*
- *Do you ask questions that demonstrate an interest in truly knowing the other person?*
- *Do you ask the kinds of questions that guide your conversation toward a deeper layer of who the other person really is?*
- *Do you repeat your point continuously?*
- *Do you get bogged down with details that aren't necessary and don't relate to their life?*

"Good listeners nurture your soul."

Take your conversation to the next level. Learn to give as well as take. You'll find yourself becoming the kind of person that others will want to be around. Ask more open-ended and in-depth questions. Look for those who have mastered the art of conversation and learn from their skills.

Cherishing Listeners

I cherish being in the company of a good listener. I have a few friends who are wonderful listeners. I love them and need them in my life. They feed my soul just by listening, and nurture me as I try to nurture them. My good listening friends know when not to say much and when to ask questions of me. They never rush me; they listen intently. On the other hand, I have other friends who may want to be good listeners, but jump in with their own stories and quickly change the conversation to themselves. The difference between these two are subtle forms of communication. But you probably have friends of both styles, just like me. While I enjoy the company of those who bring the focus to them, they don't feed and nurture my soul like the ones who listen. I want to be a nurturer of souls. If you do, then work on your listening skills. You honor people by listening to them. You'll not only be amazed by what you learn about others when you become a better listener, but also how good you end up feeling about yourself.

"You honor people by listening to them. You'll not only be amazed by what you learn about others when you become a better listener, but also how good you end up feeling about yourself."

Single Personality

How would you describe your basic personality? Would you say your most dominant personality trait is being kind, volatile, laid back, witty, serious, clingy, loud or skeptical? Are you funny, somber, cynical, gullible? Are you the humorist or the satirist? Are you "soooo nice" or so sour? Being aware of your dominant personality style will help pinpoint where and if you want to make changes. Ask your trusted friends what your personality assets are, and be prepared for their honest answers. Understanding your personality allows you to understand how you fit in the world and where you want to grow. Learn to appreciate your strengths and understand your weaknesses, it will allow you to expand your world.

Three Single Thoughts to consider

- *How will your dominating personality help you in your single life?*
- *Can it possibly work to a disadvantage?*
- *If you could strengthen one thing about yourself, what would it be?*

"Learn to appreciate your strengths and understand your weaknesses, it will allow you to expand your world."

Redesigning Your Physical Self

If your body could talk right now, what would it say about how you are treating it? The first time I asked myself that question it hit me hard. Ouch! I realized in times of crisis I need to take especially good care of myself. When things are out of sync it's easy to neglect ourselves. It takes a conscious choice to make the commitment to nurture your body and get in touch with it. Make a VOW to take better care of our body:

Your VOW to your body:

V = Vitamins, healthy eating patterns, nutrition awareness instead of unconscious eating of empty calories

O = Outlets (laughter and lasting relationships)

W = Walks (exercise and active movement)

The stress of this transition into the single life is difficult on your physical body. Keep an eye on the long-term value of a healthy active life. Now is a key time to be kind to yourself physically by engaging in healthy practices.

Venturing Out Alone

You want to make physically safe choices when you go out alone. While you want to be careful if you are a woman who goes places alone, you don't want to go to the extreme and stay home where it's safe. Organizations and clubs where people typically congregate are good places to start opening up your world.

Several times now I've said that now is the time to venture out and try new things. Everything you try won't work or be a perfect fit into your life. The good thing about failure is that we learn what works and what doesn't, we learn resilience. We learn to try again.

You can use failure as a catalyst for something that will work. Why would you want to miss out on an opportunity to laugh at yourself once in a while as you take on the world alone? Own your small failures and learn from them. It's time to start getting over yourself! Find the positive in the negative.

Following my divorce ten years ago, I thought my world had ended, when actually, it had only begun in a new and different phase. The negative in your life can be made into a positive. It will require some risks, as it took risks for me to find my current life. In so many ways, the last ten years have been the best years of my life. I love my independence, and equally, my reliance upon God. There are people I've met that I would have never known had I not become suddenly single. You, too, can turn negative situations into truly positive and wonderful experiences if you venture out to find them.

"The good thing about failure is that we learn what works and what doesn't, we learn resilience. We learn to try again."

Be Your Own Best Encourager

Create your own encouraging self-talk. Say "I can," rather than "I won't try," or "I can tolerate this rather than "this is killing me." Call yourself "Honey." (If you're a guy, you might have a hard time with this, I know. You might feel better calling yourself "friend" or "pal"). I call myself "Honey" when I talk to myself. The reasons are twofold; first, there is no one in my life calling me "honey" right now, and secondly, I have a tendency to be too hard on myself. So when I make a wrong turn, miss a deadline, or do something that wasn't the best choice, I'll say "Oh, Honey"… compassionately. It's not that I don't continue to strive for excellence, I do. It's just that I use this encouraging self-talk to stop myself from demanding perfection or beating myself up. And when new ideas and opportunities come into your life, talk to yourself. Notice your initial reaction when opportunities come up. Give yourself a moment to identify and state your exact feelings and try to understand what fear or memory this conjures up. And then proceed to encourage yourself through it if you need to.

"Instead of criticizing or judging yourself, accept your failures. Look at your unsuccessful attempts objectively with a non-condemning attitude."

Instead of criticizing or judging yourself, accept your failures. Look at your unsuccessful attempts objectively with a non-condemning attitude. Give yourself a break, take the lesson and move on. You could react with encouraging self-talk such as this;

- It was a brilliant failure don't you think?
- Didn't I totally discover the way it would not work?
- Now that I've eliminated one more method that doesn't work, I can move on to the right way to do this.

Whew, glad that's over!

Give yourself a break when you blow it. Look at the big picture. What will it matter in one hundred years or even next week, for that matter? Chances are, the mistakes can be fixed. Nobody could possibly be as hard on you as you are on yourself. Take a deep breath, smile and give yourself a break. You deserve it. What you achieve or fail to achieve is directly related to how you perceive yourself and your capabilities. Your self-talk shapes your self-perceptions. Encourage yourself whenever you hit a snag.

You are indeed going solo in a world that appears to be designed for two, but you are well on your way to your new life. Believe and know you can do this and you can do it well. You're embarking on an exciting solo life and it's all yours. Embrace it by accepting your whole self, designing your life to make it a great solo, and your own song. Take your wholeness into your whole world.

"Nobody could possibly be as hard on you as you are on yourself."

"Dance like there's nobody watching,

Love like you'll never get hurt

Sing like there's nobody listening

Live like it's heaven on earth

And speak from the heart to be heard."

William Purkey

Four Single Thoughts to Consider

- *Where do you want to go from here, and what is the first step you need to take?*
- *Identify one lesson you learned from a situation that initially appeared to be a failure.*
- *What encouraging self-talk phrase will you use to encourage yourself when you most need that support?*

Chapter 6

Dance With Your Shadow

The future holds something far greater than your past.

Facing the Past

You are being followed. Every day of every waking moment, around every corner and at every turn, you are being followed. As you stand in the light of your everyday life, you cast a shadow that follows you wherever you go. No matter how hard you try to deny it, avoid it, or run away from it, you are being followed by your own shadow. Sometimes it is evident, at other times obscure, but it is always there. The shadow I speak of is your past. Your past influences your present and affects your life today whether you realize it or not.

"Our past is the gatekeeper of our belief system. Our beliefs influence how we filter and view the world."

Our past is the gatekeeper of our belief system. Our beliefs influence how we filter and view the world. No matter how hard you may try to renounce it, your past is with you. It is something to be reckoned with and an area that needs peace. If your past was hurtful, you might be angry with it or even afraid of it. But, since it has already been a partner all of your life, make sure you have learned to dance with it.

What It Means to Dance With Your Shadow

Dancing with your shadow means recognizing your past as unchangeable, and understanding how your history has affected and moved you in the rhythm of your life. Your past doesn't have to dominate your life once you understand and deal with it. It's important that you are leading the dance.

There are several ways you can deal with your past:

You can wrestle with it. Recognize your past is there, and acknowledge that your past may pin you down from time to time.

You can despise it. Become embittered and angry over what has happened to you and stay that way for the rest of your life.

You can invite it. Blend your past with your present and use it as a forum for learning about yourself and moving on.

You can resign to it. Pretend that you are the sum of your past and there's nothing you can do about it.

You can liberate yourself from it. Design the future you want in spite of your history.

Are you aware of how your past affects your attitude,

"Dancing with your shadow means recognizing your past as unchangeable, and understanding how your history has affected and moved you in the rhythm of your life. It's important that you are leading the dance."

your self-esteem, and your relationships today? Think about your past, where you've come from. Think of words spoken and actions taken that influenced your concept of who you are and how you fit into your world.

Perhaps you have come to grips with your personal history and how it influences you today. Even so, now as you take assessment of your new life, it is a good time to reflect on where you've been and to identify past issues that influenced you. From there, you can make what adjustments you want to work on for your new life.

Meeting The Shadow

After my divorce, I went into counseling. I did so because a dear friend stated that she had gained beneficial insight from a local therapist, and the idea intrigued me. I considered myself an emotionally healthy person who had come to terms with who I was and where I was in my life. I felt I was functioning well and didn't have any real relationship issues. I had been dating a very nice man for awhile, had several close friends, and the truest test of all, my kids loved me and we got along great. It appeared that I was functioning well, yet in my interest for deeper self-knowledge, I decided to see this counselor.

Within a few sessions, I began to realize that I was indeed an amazing… mess! Where had all this stuff come from that made me who I was, without my permission? As

"Where had all this stuff come from that made me who I was, without my permission?"

I began exploring what lay deep inside me, I became a bit anxious about what else may be lurking below the surface that I did not see or realize. The crucial question for me was, to what degree was my past affecting me today? If I didn't understand and come to terms with old baggage would it sabotage my future relationships and how I relate to my world? I began to realize that how we act in relationships is based on our past beliefs. If some of our beliefs are invalid, then some of how we view our world is invalid. Unless we come to terms with who we were versus who we are becoming, we are building our world with faulty thinking and imperfect points of reference.

"If some of our beliefs are invalid, then some of how we view our world is invalid."

Voice of the Past

Here's my example of how my past met my present. Perhaps you've had a similar experience or will have one. It began in a church class as we were discussing a topic I felt strongly about. I made several statements during the class that morning, and others did as well.

Later, after the class, the service began. As I entered the sanctuary for the service I became overwhelmed with feelings of shame that I had been too outspoken in the class. After sitting for a time with tears in my eyes, I began to feel a profound warmth as an affirming thought filled my mind and heart; "The condemning voice that you hear is not the voice of your heavenly Father, it is the voice of your earthly father". It surprised me by its' contrast to what I was feeling, and a genuine feeling of calm replaced the shame. I sat there amazed at the sudden clarity of that profound truth as my past collided with my present.

During my childhood, I had heard the negative, frightening voice of my father. So many times, even as an adult, his voice seemed to still influence my thoughts and my self-talk. That strong, critical voice of my earthly father was suppressive, judgmental and accusatory. But that morning in church, the glorious overriding voice of my ultimate Father awakened me to begin a freedom from that unhealthy, demanding voice. In contrast to my past earthly father, God's gentle Spirit showed amazing love and was approachable and comforting. His Spirit was encouraging, uplifting, and possessed a gentleness that I will never forget. And He was on my side. I take great comfort in the verse below, because it identifies the same spirit that met me that morning.

"Come let us reason our case together, I even I am the one who wipes out your transgressions for My own sake. And I will not remember your sins. Put me in remembrance; let us argue our case together. State your cause, that you may be proved right, your first forefather sinned."   Isaiah 43:25

My father died when I was thirteen. Yet, I was in my late thirties when I sat in that church pew. The shadow of his disapproval followed me and influenced me all of those years. You might have a similar story of your childhood, whether the voices you heard were right or wrong, supportive or suppressive. These are your shadows. The question is, what do you do with them? How do you stop listening to invalid voices from the past so you don't sabotage yourself and future relationships? It is only by conscientiously replacing them with a new voice, a real voice of reason, truth, encouragement and peace.

I am only now beginning to grasp that losing my father at such an early age had a lasting impressionable influence on me. There was so little time for us to build a relationship. My early loss leads me to ask many questions:

"How do you stop listening to invalid voices from the past so you don't sabotage yourself and future relationships?"

Did my father's early death inadvertently and wrongly teach me the lesson that men always leave?

Did I grow up believing that men are emotionally distant and unable to fully love? Did I perceive that a man would eventually, in just a matter of time, leave me? Was my inability to let myself fully open up and love unquestionably, my defense against potential loss?

Perhaps you can search back into your own history for shadows that may have influenced your assumptions about yourself, life and relationships. I encourage you to spend some time reflecting on this highly important but often overlooked aspect of your life. What early experiences may have cast a shadow over your childhood and have you come to terms with them as an adult?

Face It

I encourage you to discern the old messages that are influencing your life. One way is to pay attention to your self-talk. Another is to review any early loss or disappointments you experienced as a child or even as an adult in your past. I encourage you to write them down in detail. Can you identify past major events that you know impacted you? Discover what originated in your past that continues to influence your thought process now, and consequently affects your relationships. With work and time, you can do this on your own, and if you need to work with a counselor awhile, I highly recommend it.

"I encourage you to spend some time reflecting on this highly important but often overlooked aspect of your life."

Four Single Thoughts to Consider
- *What favorite childhood experiences or positive teachings have helped you as an adult?*
- *How have early hurts or disappointments marked your attitude and how willing are you to talk about these experiences?*
- *Is there an area of your past that is too difficult to face or you feel you need to keep hidden?*
- *What early decisions and assumptions have you made that may have put limits on your relationship?*

We all probably suffer from our own version of negative, suppressive words in our past, those that tell us to "sit down and shut up". By recognizing past unhealthy voices and their stifling words of influence, you and I can learn to recognize and turn away from those messages that tell us to be less than what we are. The more aware we become of our own shadows, the easier it will be to recognize them in other people's attitudes and behaviors as well. We can learn how to identify the old, wrong voice in our head; and take the control of our reactions, understanding that we don't have to defy it, or react in anger once we recognize it. We can use a different point of reference in our reaction. Replace that voice of the past with a greater, healthier voice of authority, and react to this greater voice. For me, the greatest voice is the voice of God through biblical scriptures.

"The more aware we become of your own shadows, the easier it will be to recognize them in other people's attitudes and behaviors as well."

Loud Voices, Dark Shadows

You may have wondered what you do with the darkest shadows, such as abuse, trauma or shameful teachings of your past. Sometimes you can't disown them on your own, nor should you. You may think that because these events happened so many years ago they can't affect you today, but they do. I recognized in my own experience that by dealing with my issues, instead of hiding them, my life was brought to a clearer perspective. In being willing to deal with the shadows of my past, I can move the shadow to think and move more freely and clearly, and it doesn't cloud my thinking as it once did. You too can let go of those old manipulating voices. Understanding and acknowledging their presence helps bring everything out into the open, so you can understand their present hold on you. From there you can take control of, keep control of, and eventually dance with your shadow in celebration and appreciation of your rich history, good and bad, that helps make you the unique and wonderful individual that you are.

"The heart develops a particularly strong armor to protect and defend itself, but the same emotional defenses that protect us can also isolate us if they always remain up. We can only be intimate to the degree that we are willing to be open and vulnerable."

Dean Orish MD

"We yearn to be known and accepted and loved for who we are, but we get in the way of that ideal."

We know that intimacy is a basic need and a requirement for a healthy relationship. We also know that intimacy requires transparency. But sometimes we keep parts of ourselves locked up. We don't know how to get beyond our past. We yearn to be known and accepted and loved for who we are, but we get in the way of that ideal. It is because we don't understand the shadow of our past and how to deal with it (dance with it). We may hold onto our old defenses as a means of shielding ourselves against further hurt. How quickly we can become that small child full of shame if that was how our past was based. We have to face our past history honestly and courageously, and then appreciate it for the place it has in our lives.

I don't mean to make any of this sound easy. Dealing with past issues is tough. It's not a comfortable subject to face. And yet, remarkably, we are dealing with our past every day in how we're living it out. You can take the lead, or let it lead you where it wants. Open up your entire self, learn to deal with the parts of you that have put limits on your potential and your relationships. Take the step toward controlling your shadow rather than it controlling you. You choose the music, you name the dance.

"Dealing with past issues is tough. And yet, remarkably, we are dealing with our past every day in how we're living it out. You can take the lead, or let it lead you where it wants."

Vibrations of Childhood

I asked Peter, a psychotherapy professor at a dinner one night if we ever truly get over our childhood. He put his hands on the table and shook it gently. He said childhood is like a vibration that is always present, and for some of us, it vibrates gently, but for others, it shakes violently. He said there is every possible variation in between those two extremes, but to some extent, it is always there. If what Peter says is true, how can we possibly ignore the affects our past has on us and how can it not influence the way we relate to our world and relationships with others?

My friend Jane, a Licensed Professional Counselor, who specializes in childhood attachment disorders, says that our bonding capability is based upon our first few months of life. Healthy bonding occurs when mother or caregiver provides ample touching, cuddling, and nurturing. If, for some reason, this has not occurred, these individuals can be adversely affected their entire lives. Without this imperative bonding, those individuals often become fearful and defensive. Some will actually react violently to those who attempt to get near to them. It's hard to fathom that babies can be so intensely, emotionally fragile. It's equally hard to fathom the lifelong impact of those early months of life. Perhaps it gives credence to why some people can be cruel or controlling, while others are natural at bonding and forming relationships.

Five Single Thoughts to Consider

- *What prominent personality trait do you see as a result of your past, whether favorable or unfavorable?*
- *In what way have you either cultivated or minimized that behavior?*
- *What healthy relationships did you have early on in your life that allowed you to have healthy relationships now?*
- *What is, in your view, the most obvious shadow from your past?*
- *How has it influenced your attitude and actions in relationships?*

Psychologists agree that in our intimate relationships, we unknowingly choose an image of our parents, even if it is unhealthy. In my life, my relationship with my father, and also the relationship with my husband were shadows I had to recognize and then come to terms with. Only then was I able to dance with that part of my history. As a result, I began experiencing healthier, more equal relationships. Slowly, I learned that not all men wanted to leave me, use negative energy against me, squelch me, control me, or want me to sit down and shut up. I discovered that some of them were healthy and mature enough to want to know and love me. I've found that men come in all variety of shapes, sizes and ideas, and not all of them are like my images of the past. Dancing with my shadow is the first step in reinventing my relationship images.

"Dancing with my shadow is the first step in reinventing my relationship images."

Conversing With Your Past

I invite you to sit down and converse with your past. Find and examine the shadows that have held you back or interfered with your ability to enjoy rewarding and healthy relationships. Your shadows will be there, lurking within some of the expectations you feel obligated to meet, inspiring reactions and thought processes you use, they are your negative or positive voices of encouragement or suppression. Your shadows are talking to you, whether you acknowledge them or not. Talk back to them so you can face the entirety of your life: healthy, unhealthy, happy, unhappy and more. Learn to diffuse any old unhealthy patterns you may have.

Find a counselor or the engaging ear of a trusted friend so you can walk through this conversation. Too many of us do a good job of hiding the hurts of our past.

Denial doesn't work. I'll be the first to admit that conversing with these intricate parts of ourselves isn't easy after so many years of working so hard to conceal them. But engaging with your past allows you to break that self-perpetuating cycle of old patterns.

Otherwise, the next partner in your life will be the same type of person you've chosen in the past. I'm sure you've heard of the woman who marries the "same man" over and over again, the only difference is the DNA profile.

"Denial doesn't work. I'll be the first to admit that conversing with these intricate parts of ourselves isn't easy after so many years of working so hard to conceal them."

Is There An Innocent Party?

I've concluded that even though I was not the one to end my marriage, several of the marriage issues were mine. Perhaps I had shut down and waited for him to leave. In fact, maybe I expected him to leave, because he was so much like my emotionally distant father. In choosing him, had I set myself up for a familiar situation with a man who would always be emotionally unavailable? True enough, my husband had his own issues that contributed to the failure of the marriage, but I also contributed.

In finding that his love was inaccessible, I shut down. I probably shut down during my marriage just as I had in my childhood home life. I did it to protect myself, to survive. I can now look at my past behavior and determine if that's how I want to be in my future life. I'm not suggesting you analyze your past to death, but to reflect on how your past has influenced you.

Decide what you will and will not perpetuate. Take a long look at the ways your past affected the relationship you just came from. It is vital to the start of a new healthy life, that you are aware of how your history affects your actions and maybe more importantly, your reactions. Once freed from those shadows, you and I are not as prone to be manipulated by our past.

"Decide what you will and will not perpetuate."

Single Thought to Consider

- *In some ways we contributed to the relationship that ended in a divorce. How can you lovingly forgive yourself for the part you played?*

For those of us who have experienced divorce or the end of a significant relationship, it's helpful to understand that we all behave in ways that for some reason make sense to us. Consider also, that people who hurt you (intentionally or not) come from their own culture, with shadows of their own.

Single Thought to consider
- *What did you see in your mate that could have possibly been a result of his or her childhood or past?*

Dancing With the Past

There she was, the little flower girl on the wedding dance floor, dancing all by herself, her white dress floating around her as she twirled with her arms outstretched. Sometimes her hands would reach upward as her shoulders and body flowed with the pulse of the music. It seemed as if she was riding on the rhythm. She didn't notice anyone around her. She was just an innocent little girl with a free spirit who just had to dance. The music was her companion and her shadow spilled across the dance floor. She danced with such abandon and freedom. Don't we all long to have that freedom, especially over our past? That little girl was my granddaughter at my daughter's wedding, but more importantly, she is a picture of the spirit inside of us that longs to be innocent again, innocent and uninhibited enough to find the freedom to dance.

Celebrate all of who you are, not in spite of your past, but because of it. Again, look at the compassion it

"Don't we all long to have that freedom, especially over our past? The spirit inside of us longs to be innocent again, innocent and uninhibited enough to find the freedom to dance."

allows you to feel toward others. You can become an authentic person that relates to others because of what you experienced in your past. What you have overcome is part of what makes you the incredible person you are today. Take the lessons you've so profoundly learned as you take your past lightly. The dance will flow and you will take the lead. Dance with your shadow, it has already been your partner all of your life.

"Dance with your shadow, it has already been your partner all of your life."

Chapter 7

Finances

"Until you make peace with who you are, you'll never be content with what you have."

Doris Mortman

A divorce or the death of a spouse alters your finances dramatically and it is important to look at money issues with a clear perspective to make the right decisions. As we well know, the simple definition of financial management is how much comes in versus what goes out. Yet many people (both single and married), seriously struggle with budgets and their spending patterns. Emotional turmoil can spin our finances out of control very quickly.

Unless you are a financial planner or have kept abreast of the financial world, you will need to take extra precautions when making financial decisions during this transitional period. I am by no means a financial advisor, but over the past decade I've learned that many of our financial troubles are not always about the numbers. Many times, our financial troubles are a result of our attitude, beliefs, and our unwillingness to put some desires on hold to secure a better future.

Until You Control Your Money, You Cannot Control Your Life

Finances dictate so much of our lives that it is imperative to control spending so that we don't lose control of our lives. Following a divorce or a spouse's death it's tempting to use this hurting time as an excuse to become "emotional purchasers". In other words, we make a decision to buy based on our feelings and emotional needs instead of facts and physical needs. Men do it and women do it. Sometimes when we hurt, we might spend money to mask the pain. We may spend because we feel our life is out of control and empty, and we attempt to regain control and fill our lives by buying things and acquiring new possessions.

"We can't buy our way out of pain."

Flashing that charge card allows a sense of power at a time when we often feel powerless. Our reasoning may include: "I deserve it", "I'll show them!" "Maybe if I buy this for myself it will perk me up and I won't feel so sad". But we can't buy our way out of pain. Even though we may think we deserve to treat ourselves, or revenge our ex-spouse, or prove we have some control over our life, this is a lose/lose strategy. Spending will never resolve our issues nor help us heal. Buying things may provide an outlet or a temporary distraction to avoid the deep issues of life and what's truly happening to us, but these good feelings won't last. And the saddest part is society (i.e., charge card companies) make it so easy to lose that control.

It is essential to remember that spending patterns should not be driven by our moods. Take note of your emotions when you're buying something and ask yourself some straightforward questions:

Why am I buying this item?

Am I trying to meet an emotional need

or fill a void?

It doesn't matter how hard you try or how much you buy, material things can't fill the void within you. If your finances are already precarious, emotional purchases can exacerbate your current money problems.

Once we understand our tendency to purchase things we can start curbing the habit to "feed" our emotions. We need to know when we're doing it, and why, so we can bring ourselves back to reality. It is useless to think that you can control your life without controlling your money. To improve your financial decision-making, it may help to seek the counsel of trustworthy experts during this time. Look for free options first (banks, knowledgeable friends, books, television programs and articles on financial management). If you need further advice, consider meeting with a professional. The money you spend could end up

"It is useless to think that you can control your life without controlling your money."

being a valuable investment.

Be aware, that times of transition or emotional upheaval are often times of great financial vulnerability. Be cautious if anyone approaches you with big promises of what their services or products can do for you. Divorces and deaths are public knowledge, and unfortunately there are those who consider the suddenly single as potential customers. Be cautious of financial services or debt consolidators who work only to postpone your debt without addressing your financial management issues. It is possible that using these services could damage your credit rating as much as a bankruptcy.

> "Be aware, that times of transition or emotional upheaval are often times of great financial vulnerability."

Three Single Thoughts to Consider

- *What is your biggest area of financial vulnerability?*
- *What is the largest debt that you currently carry?*
- *Who is your confidant on financial matters?*

If There Was Ever A Time To Be Conservative, It Is Now

Be cautious. Be patient. Lay low. You'll be rewarded down the road by playing it smart now. As a general rule, don't make any big decisions during the first year on your own, unless absolutely necessary. Examples of big decisions include moving, changing jobs, renovating the house, purchasing a new car, or other big-ticket items. Let the dust of your transition settle first. Conduct a financial assessment of where you are now and keep yourself in a holding pattern. Use the first year to focus on healing, self-development and discovering who you are now as a single person. Limit your expenses as much as possible, and keep in mind that your expenses will not be shared or paid off by another person. It's all up to you now. Money is all about perspective; less of it requires creativity and refocusing on what's important. Focus on the things of life that matter beyond the material.

Finding Your Financial Motto

Shortly after my separation, I went to a craft show at the local high school. This was a very chaotic time for me. We were finalizing the divorce, and I was trying to figure out where I stood in many areas, including finances. I attended the craft show alone, sensing that "pit in the stomach feel" that accompanied me so frequently in those early days. I had very little money and everything in my life was up in the air and uncertain. I found a small wooden plaque at the craft show that read "Live Within Your Harvest". It resonated with me as my financial solution and my financial motto. I decided to make it my new financial motto for the single life. If I could heed this simple advice and only spend what I "harvested" (or earned), using little or no credit, I could make it. I could save myself the heartache that out-of-control debt leads to.

"Live Within Your Harvest"

Having a motto to focus on and refer to, helped me gain in strength and confidence. Even today, that plaque sits on my refrigerator as a reminder, that with the right attitude I can make it financially as a single person.

Short Term Pleasure or Long Term Joy?

In a way, budgets are like diets and I sometimes struggle with both. Each can feel confining, but both are necessary for a healthier future. Instead of focusing on what I can't have, I choose to think that wise spending is powerful and gives me control of my life, instead of being controlled by bills. Well handled finances, like eating smart, will take care of you in the long term and give you the rewards of a healthy life.

"Instead of focusing on what I can't have, I choose to think that wise spending is powerful and gives me control of my life, instead of being controlled by bills."

Here's a good question to ask yourself before you buy something: Do I see this item in the "big picture frame" of my life and with the future in mind, or is this for monetary pleasure or escape? I'm not saying don't spend money on yourself, or not to be frivolous once in a while with small indulgences, if there is room in the budget. But for now, it is wise to decide which purchases are really necessary. Consider how your spending habits may need to change with your new budget. Remember, where you are now is temporary. It's a passage. And you'll get through it faster and smoother if this passage is free of a heavy debt load. It might be helpful to label potential purchases as what you must have (essentials), what you would like to have (optional), and what you dream to have (rewards for yourself).

To gain a better foothold on your finances, kick your credit card to the curb. Pay with cash and checks as much as possible instead of using the credit card. That will help limit those impulse purchases that will come back to haunt you. Debit cards may appear to give you tighter control on your finances, but be aware that you can debit yourself into insufficient funds and overdraft fees. Debit cards do not shut off at zero dollars. By staying in tight control of your credit and debit balances you can keep yourself out of financial trouble. Closely monitor your check registry and verify your account transactions with on-line banking.

Three Single Thoughts to Consider

- *What would you describe as your biggest financial weakness?*
- *How can you discipline yourself to avoid the places or circumstances that tempt you to spend money you don't have?*
- *What restraint or financial motto can you use to help you think through any purchases that exceed $50.00 or $100.00?*

"To gain a better foothold on your finances, kick your credit card to the curb. Pay with cash and checks as much as possible instead of using a the credit card. "

Small Deliberate Steps

Thinking long term may be the last thing on your mind right now. You may feel as if you're barely surviving this trying time. However, the long term is not as far away as you think, regardless of your age. Small deliberate steps make for long lasting results. Just think, one payment at a time eventually erases debt. My dear friend Mike taught me that when we face huge obstacles in life to remember how you would eat an elephant (if you were so inclined). You would eat it one bite at a time. For our purposes, debt is taken care of one payment at a time. If you can control your short term spending, you are controlling your long-term rewards. Don't trade short-lived instant gratification for your long-term joy and security.

"If you can control your short term spending, you are controlling your long-term rewards."

I remember the incredible feeling of walking into the mortgage company and making the final payment on my house as a single mother on a modest income. There is nothing that can match the feeling - no new car smell, no cruise, no bigger house, no closet full of clothes, nothing. There was no big hurrah from the world, no awards ceremony. But quietly, and persistently I won a major victory. My discipline paid off, literally. Paying off my mortgage gave me a sense of satisfaction and control over my life.

If I can do it, you can do it. If something like this seems at all overwhelming, (as it is for most of us) just think small deliberate steps (remember the elephant). In the same way, you conquer debt by small steps. Don't neglect the fact that you can also sink deeply into debt by making too many undisciplined small purchases. I know the "shopping trance" we can put ourselves into, and it can be difficult to come to our senses. Consider the long term. Focus on the outcome; financial freedom in the future and the satisfaction of being out of debt. Picture yourself being in control, knowing that even if you lost your job you could survive because, unlike the majority, you have your finances under control and a debt load that is manageable.

For the first year or two a good rule to live by is this: If I can't purchase it with cash, then I can't afford it. Make that statement a part of your suddenly single new life, so you won't go further in debt and find yourself suddenly broke.

A New Mindset

Here's one way to reframe your thinking toward purchasing. Consider how your shopping habits would change if you were to compare the items you buy to the actual hours you spend at your job to pay for them. Realistically, you should figure your net income. Imagine a meter on every item calculating your hourly wage and how long you'd have to work to pay for it. Or imagine a clock hanging in your office that displayed what item you are

"If I can't purchase it with cash, then I can't afford it. Make that statement a part of your suddenly single new life, so you won't go further in debt and find yourself suddenly broke."

working for every hour of the workday. If you realized that each of your purchases equaled time of your life, whether big-ticket items or small, would your spending habits change? Would you alter some of your purchases? If you saw a new car as sixteen hours of labor per week, or your house as trading three days of your life per week, would you still want to make the commitment?

Single Income Mindset

You are now living with one income to sustain you. Spending that income boils down to exchanging your life for a dollar. Perhaps, you already know where the money goes. If not, or if you'd like to get a better understanding of it visually, make a log of your bills. For me it was simplest to have it all on one sheet under a column with headings for each monthly pay date. This can be done on an excel spreadsheet or paper and pencil. Make your visual chart an overview of that time period and watch where your money is going over the next six months.

"Can you keep spending at this pace?"

Simultaneously, take the next two weeks and track every item you buy: groceries, coffee, fast food, transportation and so on. This gives you a clear idea of where your money goes. Can you keep spending at this pace? Are there small things you could give up (cappuccino, cigarettes, fast food, high priced brand name goods) that could add up to an extra house payment over a year's time? Can you visualize how an extra house payment now and then could have a long-term impact? Awareness exercises such as this can help you strategize how to make changes for the long term so you can reap the benefits. If you are fortunate to receive extra income, such as a work bonus, or profit sharing, your first impulse may be to spend it on something fun. But if your vision is to be debt free and in control, consider putting that extra money on the principal of your mortgage or a Roth IRA, ensuring some security for the future.

Building Your Network

If you haven't already done so, establish your financial relationships as quickly as possible. Don't be afraid to ask for advice and get to know your banker. How? Go in and introduce yourself. Sit down and meet some of the bank managers or representatives. Instead of dealing with strangers, develop a relationship with a real person and a real financial institution. Build your relationships early. Determine which bank or credit union is most receptive and friendly. Explain your situation. Tell them who you are and what you need from them. They will be eager to tell you about their services and help assess where you are now financially.

Of course, you have dealt with banks for years, but perhaps not on your own. It helps to have a trustworthy resource, because you never know when you might have

"If you haven't already done so, establish your financial relationships as quickly as possible."

a need. Most major banks are full service banks and this means they can assist you in saving, investing, and financial advising. Some banks will even help you with the basics of balancing your checkbook if you ever needed it. They can advise you on investments and retirement, or account reviews.

Set aside time to work on your financial network. Take a morning or the whole day to meet with a few banks, credit unions, or financial advisors to determine how they can assist you. Note how they treat you and how much time they are willing to give you. This might indicate how easy they will be to work with in the future.

"Note how they treat you and how much time they are willing to give you. This might indicate how easy they will be to work with in the future."

Banks have confidentiality rules. Hopefully the accounts you currently have are no longer joint accounts. If you do co-own something with your ex spouse (which astonishingly happens frequently), I strongly advise terminating these arrangements because both of you have 100% rights to the account. You have the right to close a joint account. From there, you can proceed to open an individual account (in your name only). No matter how amicable your divorce or situation is, I highly recommend that you do not use a joint account after the divorce.

If you have no credit rating, you must establish credit in your own name. If there is a loan or mortgage that is under both of your names, you cannot just simply remove one person's name off the loan. You will have to refinance and take on a new loan in your own name. Be prepared, this may result in a different interest rate, which you will need to factor into your budget.

If you think you might be running into financial trouble, be proactive. Your first instinct may be to ignore the problem, to postpone dealing with it, or to deny it. This will only make things worse. Take charge. Let your banker (the one you've established a relationship with) know that you are in need of some assistance, guidance and direction. Help is available. Your situation is not unique in the financial world. Things happen. If you see desperate times coming, go to your banker. Be open, forthright and honest. Not all banks and credit unions are the cold hard institutions you may believe them to be. Your bank representative may be able to devise a workable plan.

From time to time, we all make financial mistakes. I certainly made a few. That is why it is smart to do your homework and ask questions to minimize errors in judgment. Be cautious of potentially costly decisions such as taking out a bridge loan. Don't sign papers without understanding the small print, with big ramifications. Be watchful of "set up" or administrative fees.

When I bought my second house, I thought it was a good idea to get a bridge loan because I was transitioning homes across the state. That meant for a period of time, I owned two homes, which is a real burden for a single woman

"If you see desperate times coming, go to your banker. Be open, forthright and honest. Your bank representative may be able to devise a workable plan."

and not a smart move to make. It was the relationship with my banker that helped me out of it when I needed an immediate loan of $5000 to close on the home I sold. This could not have been so readily available without my having established an earlier relationship with the bank manager.

What You Want to Know About Credit Ratings

Have you established credit in your name? How good is your credit? Do you know your FICO score? Your FICO score is a financial score banks use to determine how much of a credit risk you may be. The higher your score the better it is for you since it will make your interest rates lower.

"Keep your credit rating squeaky clean as you venture into the single life."

Keep your credit rating squeaky clean as you venture into the single life. This is motivation to close those accounts and be financially independent from your former spouse. Even if he or she has promised to make the payments on a joint loan, because your name is on the loan, you are still responsible for the balance. If the payments aren't made, a negative mark will show up on your credit report for years to come. In most circumstances you may need to make payments rather than face the negative consequences. Let me remind you how vital it is to make your house payments, student loans and charge account payments on time. These three are the most influential criteria when it comes to your credit rating. And your bill paying patterns will influence your mortgage interest rates, as well as your ability to receive a quick signature loan when or if you need one.

Protect Your Credit Rating At All Costs

After moving from my country home to a nearby town closer to my job, I learned a hard lesson about credit ratings from my former phone company. I won't name the company, but I will tell you its title consists of three letters and leave it at that. Not realizing, when I moved into a different area code that I kept my phone number from our previous area code, for my computer line. Between myself, an avid user of the Internet and my teenage daughter as well, we used the computer every day, and well into the night.

We were now unknowingly using long distance phone service. My first phone bill was $900. After I changed to a local number, I received a second bill for $600. I contacted the phone company explaining my mistake, begging for a one-time forgiveness for the debt, or at least a grace period to give me time to pay; they refused. Quite honestly, they did not care. They had a "gotcha" attitude. The only thing they did allow me was to make two payments a month instead of one, while issuing me a measly $25 credit.

I had to pay this massive bill of $1500.00 for less

than two month's worth of telephone privileges! That was a financial nightmare for me and it hurt. But my credit rating was, and will always be, incredibly important. As a single woman determined to be independent, I paid it. I paid it angrily, and reluctantly - but I paid it.

Working in the service industry as a marketing and account manager for businesses, I know the benefits of treating people fairly. Obviously, I changed my long distance phone company. By losing me as a customer, this unnamed communication company lost far more than that $1500. Regardless, I understood the importance of good credit and I needed to protect my financial reputation. Not paying that bill would have resulted in higher costs in the long run because of higher interest rates and/or extra charges and fees I would have had to pay in the future.

"My credit rating was, and will always be, incredibly important. As a single woman determined to be independent, I paid it. I paid it angrily, and reluctantly - but I paid it."

Three Single Thoughts to Consider
- *What is your five year financial goal?*
- *Have you created a written plan for achieving your goals?*
- *What is one thing you can do right now to start working toward your financial goals?*

A Few Thoughts on Investing

Before you consider investing for your future, protect your present life by having a cash reserve of three to six months living expenses tucked away in case of an emergency, such as illness or job loss. Then you are truly ready to start investing. Every person should have a 401K or an IRA plan. This is true for self-employed individuals as well. If you do not, you are literally throwing away money due to the tax savings available to you. If finances are tight, let your contributions to these plans drop temporarily if you need to, but don't borrow from your 401K unless it is absolutely necessary. If you must borrow from it, make sure you understand all the liabilities you may accrue in taxes and government penalties. It is not profitable to allocate 10-20% of your income if you have to go back and borrow from your investment savings. Find a contribution amount that works for you and then forget the money is there until you retire.

"When you're on your own, you must plan for your future. Don't put it off or believe someone else will secure your future for you. It's time to plan your own."

Make your contributions to your 401K and IRA modest and reasonable during this transition so you can live without the money you contribute. The Roth IRA allows you to contribute after tax dollars and accrues interest as nontaxable income. These two basic plans make up what I call, "my old lady fund", and I just hope I'm fortunate to use it someday. When you're on your own, you must plan for your future. Don't put it off or believe someone else will secure your future for you. It's time to plan your own.

Financial advisors can help you determine your investment personality and advise accordingly. Some advisors work by the hour and some are paid commissions for what they sell. If you had already established long-term investments when you were married, revisit your advisor to ensure you trust this person with your revised financial future. A past financial advisor may know your history, but now that you're on your own, this same individual may not be the match you'd like in your life right now. Determine if you wish to sever any other ties with professionals who assisted you and your spouse, such as your tax preparer or accountant. You now have the responsibility to make these decisions.

Once you decide who will be your advisor, you'll need to choose what type of investments to put your money in. A good banker or financial advisor will instruct you on how to proceed. Some banks will work with you for free, but advisors usually charge you for a portfolio assessment. Make sure you have a clear outline of expectations and the fees you will be charged. Be wary of working with anyone who contacts or approaches you. It is you who should make the initial contact. Ask your financially savvy friends for their recommendation, then listen to your gut instead of a sales pitch before you select anything. It is your future at stake.

"Determine if you wish to sever any other ties with professionals who assisted you and your spouse, such as your tax preparer or accountant. You now have the responsibility to make these decisions."

Saving for Your Children's College

If you have dependent children, one savings plan you may be concerned with is college costs for those children.

Don't make the assumption that your former spouse has the same views for your children's financial future and college as you do. It would be nice to assume that both of you will share responsibility for college costs. If you are a woman whose primary focus has been home making, you may also assume the father will take a larger portion of this responsibility. Be aware that you may be headed for disappointment. Unfortunately, divorce can do peculiar things to attitudes toward responsibilities. Prepare yourself that you may be the only parent that is committed to your child's future. There is no legal responsibility for any parent to provide for the cost of higher education. The Roth IRA, mentioned earlier allows a way to save for college costs with tax advantages. If you have not already started, I'd suggest looking into it. I state this for your benefit, since it will influence your financial future as well as theirs.

The Required Skills of Tracking and Negotiating

Bill tracking methods will vary for all of us. Some of us use spreadsheets to track expenses while others will use the Internet to process transactions. Some will prefer sending payments or even making their payments in person. The method doesn't matter. Do what works best for you or is the most comfortable. I created my own system, the "chip clip" method. I use those potato chip clips that hold the bags closed. I'm quite certain you will never see this

"The bill tracking method you select doesn't matter. Use the system that works best for you or is the most comfortable."

method used by any financially savvy person, nor will this system be reported in a financial magazine, but it works for me. I put all the bills in a chip clip, in order of their due date. When my paycheck arrives I pay the bills. And I thank God when the chip clip is empty, because that means I can pay my bills. Assess your system and see if it needs revising. It's a subject few of us discuss, and yet, some of us could use some help with it. Do whatever it takes that allows you to pay those bills on time. You can also check into convenience services such as online banking and automatic payment plans. What's important is that you are comfortable with the system you choose, and you keep your credit in line.

"Some of us become squeamish when it comes to negotiating. Being able to discuss money, price and fees is vital in the business world and it's essential in your personal world too."

Three Single Thoughts to Consider

- *Where did you learn your financial management skills and philosophies (parents, spouse, college)?*
- *Which ones have worked for you in the past and which ones have been detrimental?*
- *Where is the first place you need to focus to get your finances in order?*

Negotiating

Some of us become squeamish when it comes to negotiating. Being able to discuss money, price and fees is vital in the business world and it's essential in your personal world too. If you're like many of us, your negotiating skills may need sharpening, so get ready for opportunities to practice them. They are most certainly coming! For the suddenly single, it may be difficult negotiating in areas where you lack experience, such as roofs, furnace repair, buying a new car, etc. The key is not being afraid to ask questions again and again until you fully understand your options. Try to look at all of the alternatives, perhaps not evident at first glance. Some options may not be volunteered by the business you are dealing with because they're less profitable to them.

The point is that you must be willing to look after your own personal business of finances. There are times to be creative and proactive and not take the usual means of business for granted. Explore your options and pursue alternatives. Once you understand all of your options you can then negotiate. Does your roof need to be redone? Don't go with the first estimate; get three or four. Choose the lowest bid and take it to the person you really want to do the work to see if they will beat the lowest bid. Make sure they are reputable. Ask for reliable references or contact the Better Business Bureau. See if there have been any complaints against the company you want to employ.

You can negotiate with just about anyone: roofers, plumbers, home construction, car salespeople, realtors, even sometimes in stores, particularly if an item is on clearance,

"The point is that you must be willing to look after your own personal business of finances. There are times to be creative and proactive and not take the usual means of business for granted."

slightly damaged, or poorly packaged. Negotiating is a skill that we all need to know and it could be vital to your financial survival. Negotiating takes a willingness to ask, and it's worth the risk. It's a skill you will use often in business and in your personal life. It certainly trains you in tact, communication skills, and getting what you want. The worst the other party can say is "no". But it's worth the risk to get one "yes" to really make it pay off.

Using Plastic

"Negotiating is a skill that we all need to know and it could be vital to your financial survival."

Credit cards are a temptation most people can't refuse, and credit card companies are playing a game that only they can win. Pay attention when using your credit cards and resist the temptation to put your future at risk. A Frontline program on PBS stated that 35 million Americans pay only the minimum payment on their credit card. Even at the lowest percentage interest rate, if you pay only the minimum, you will never pay off your credit card debt!

Credit card companies have the liberty to change your interest rate at will, thanks to the "universal default" clause. If you miss a payment, or are late on a payment to another creditor, your interest rate can be changed arbitrarily by credit card companies. Read the small print. Scrutinize your statements. Your FICO score will determine how much interest you will pay on your credit card, your mortgage and maybe even what you pay for rent.

Knowledge is power. Awareness is the name of the game. Details you may have overlooked in the past will require your utmost attention now. Although you have a multitude of things to monitor and solely be responsible for already, you cannot afford to stay uninformed when it comes to money matters.

When you purchase anything on credit and finance it at high interest, you are paying additional costs of hundreds of dollars per year. Minimum monthly payments will increase the years you'll be in debt. We may know this, but somehow that reality eludes us when we shop and we want something. That "I want it now" philosophy is taking your future dollars and your future away from you. Revise your thinking to be guided by the phrase "need to", instead of "want to". You work too hard to give your earnings to a credit card company. Put that same money into a mutual fund and it will yield personal wealth and security for you. Think about where the real value is. Even if someplace is offering the greatest sale ever, if you have to pay high interest and years of payments, it is not really a sale at all. Can you really afford to save any more money shopping those sales? Define what really adds to your life and understand the truth that charging with credit takes away from your life.

"Knowledge is power. Details you may have overlooked in the past will require your utmost attention now."

Home Buying

Even though I've suggested that you resist making major purchases during the first year or two of suddenly becoming single, sometimes it may be necessary. If you must make a major purchase, here are some things you want to know. In my view, fixed interest mortgages are the best. Definitely avoid the ARM or "interest only" loans. A 30-year fixed mortgage might be ideal for you, especially because you can always pay more on the principal at any time, but if finances get tight you can at least make the more reasonable payments.

If you buy a house or take on a mortgage, be aware of the impact you can make by adding extra money onto each payment during the first few years of the mortgage. Those extra dollars go directly on the principle. You will literally save thousands of dollars in interest and pay off your loan years earlier. That's what happened with me and its one of the reasons I could walk into my mortgage company and write that last house payment. The common notion is that you will lose out on the tax write offs. You can consult your financial advisor for advice on this issue, but it just doesn't make sense to pay out money to get a portion of it back. The following three sentences may open your eyes to what I'm suggesting.

"If you buy a house or take on a mortgage, be aware of the impact you can make by adding extra money onto each payment during the first few years of the mortgage."

"Take a $75,000 loan at 10% interest amortized for 30 yrs. By adding $25 every month to the regular $658 payment, you will reduce the term of the loan by more than five years. The extra $7400 you invest will knock off $34,000 of what you'd otherwise have to pay."

Source: Changing Times

Woman are Big Buyers

According to the National Association of Realtors, in 2005 single women purchased one of every five homes sold. That's nearly 1.5 million home purchases - more than twice the number purchased by single men. If you are a single woman, you are part of a viable market. Keep in mind that divorced and widowed women who purchase a home may be considered "first time buyers" even if they bought homes with their spouses. This may qualify you for further help such as receiving down payment assistance or low payment loans. Find a banker who will take the time to educate you on all the possibilities.

"It doesn't matter how much money you make, what matters is how you spend it."

"But ah! Think what you do when you run into debt, you give another power over your liberty."

Benjamin Franklin

Almost as wise as Ben was my grandfather-in-law, Grandfather Moses (yes, that was his name!). He used to say that it doesn't matter how much money you make, what matters is how you spend it. This also includes how much you save for your future. I took his words to heart and hope you will too.

You might be thinking as you read this chapter, that it's not so much a lack of discipline as a lack of the paycheck amount! I understand. Sometimes circumstances don't allow you to budget precisely. Raising teenagers is a perfect example of grappling with the inexact science of unplanned financial needs. They spontaneously spring expenses on you that cannot possibly be predicted, along with necessary expenses such as school, sports and activities. It is nearly impossible to precisely control those unknown, unexpected expenses. However, devising a plan with guidelines at least gives you a foundation to work with. You can budget an amount for the "teenage unexpected". Along the way, just as you had to learn it, teach your children the difference between a need and a want. They need to hear "no" once in a while, just like we all do in the real world. Learning financial discipline will help them become better people.

"Devising a plan with guidelines at least gives you a foundation to work with."

In the early years, when our children were very young, we had very little money. We would go to McDonald's after church and I'd tell my kids, "You can have fries or a soda with your hamburger, but you can't have both". It touches my heart that they recall this experience with no anguish or resentment. Along with the homemade Halloween costumes and Popsicles in the park, they smile at the memories we had. It was actually good for my children to be exposed to limits on their choices. They needed to hear "no". The key is how you present your "no" and the limitations you set. Teach them discretion as a challenge or a game, and show them the thrill of a bargain. Teach them that life is all about the discipline of choices, and keeping the big picture in mind.

"If you want your children to turn out well, spend twice as much time with them, and half as much money on them."

Abigail Van Buren

Finances are the one area in which you cannot afford to be emotional or careless. Yes, it's frustrating at times and you need extreme diligence to manage your money. If you're going to get frustrated, direct your frustration and anger toward those who shamelessly make money off unsuspecting consumers. Take that anger and funnel it toward cultivating discipline in your spending and saving patterns. I don't know how much sudden singlehood has caused you to change your lifestyle because of money, but I rarely meet a single woman or man who isn't greatly affected financially by divorce or a premature death. I cannot emphasize enough the need to be wise with money at this critical time. Your future is at risk. If you are wise and disciplined, you can make this transition a smoother and shorter one. Again, live within your harvest, and you will have the joy of future harvests to reap.

"Finances are the one area in which you cannot afford to be emotional or careless."

The Giving Circle of Life

All this being said, here's one last thought on finances. For balance in our lives, it is important that we find someplace to contribute that is greater than ourselves. We need a cause that we believe in. Perhaps it's your church, your school or a favorite community agency. You can contribute time or money, or both. It is not necessarily the amount as much as it is the act of giving. Life is about giving and receiving, and when we give so that other people's lives are enriched, we find that we have enriched our own. And in doing so, we complete the giving circle of life. Even as you watch out for your financial future, always look for and find a way to contribute to something greater than yourself.

"Life is about giving and receiving, and when we give so that other people's lives are enriched, we find that we have enriched our own."

Chapter 8

Lessons Learned in the Dating World

"I have a friend. I sing louder. I smile bigger. I laugh harder. I pray more. I love better.

Nicole Johnson

Playing the Field... Where's the Field?

When I was first divorced, a co-worker of mine made the comment, "Well, Kathey, I guess you'll be playing the field now." I responded, "Harrison, it's been twenty years and I don't even know where the field is!" I have since found the field of dating. It is expansive, diverse and sometimes mysterious. The field has a few snakes in it, but for the most part, delightful people and wonderful surprises. I never intended to chronicle any of my relationships nor did I imagine they would be such rich learning experiences, but indeed they were. The lessons I've learned in dating relate to all of us who find ourselves suddenly single. I hope they will help prepare you for what you will face in

"The lessons I've learned in dating relate to all of us who find ourselves suddenly single."

the dating world. Most of all, I hope these lessons learned will help raise your awareness of red flags, or warning signs indicating unhealed or unhealthy people. The whole point is to avoid making the same mistake over and over again.

Getting Ready

The natural tendency for many single people is to believe that the next relationship is the ultimate answer to finding true happiness. There was a time when I honestly believed that. After having several relationships since my divorce, I've come to believe that true happiness is not the result of the next relationship. True happiness is the result of finding peace within yourself, your place in God and nurturing your bonds of friendship. I don't want to discourage you from desiring a relationship. However, I do hope you'll be cautious, because the failure statistics of second and third marriages are too high to be ignored.

Are you searching for the perfect mate, or are you searching for the perfect self and peace within that self? Are you seeking wholeness of yourself in other people? Relationships are a vital part of a balanced life and this includes friends and acquaintances, not just someone you date. Nourish the intimate relationships you have now, without feeling that you can only be complete by seeing yourself in another exclusive relationship.

I left this important chapter on dating toward the

"Are you searching for the perfect mate, or are you searching for the perfect self and peace within that self? Are you seeking wholeness of yourself in other people?"

end of this book for a reason. I'm hoping you won't go there (in the field) until you're truly ready. To be ready is to take care of your old business first. Wait until you've resolved the transitional issues (or at least gotten them under control). You've come to terms with your circumstances, you have forgiven the ex husband/wife, the kids are taken care of and your finances are relatively in order. You've established that you are a whole person, not half of anything, or a pending couple waiting to be complete. You are in the process of defining who you are and where you want to go next in your life. You are learning to redefine and recapture your dreams and go after them. Because you are taking care of your old business, the result is a fuller understanding of who you are. In essence, you are preparing yourself for a new life. In this stage of your transition, you will become stronger and more content. You won't need to desperately search outside yourself for significance.

The Most Vital Relationship

It is my belief that our value is found more in knowing who we are in God's design than in establishing the next relationship. Start your new life by finding the strengths and gifts that God gave you to find your life's dreams. That is the key to your happiness. It's not another person making you whole. The only relationship that can fully complete us is the one with our Creator. There is no

"In this stage of your transition, you will become stronger and more content. You won't need to desperately search outside yourself for significance."

substitute. In fact, we sometimes search in a human being for that which only God can fill. Finding your peace comes in finding God first, through a relationship with His Son, Jesus Christ. I'm not speaking of the practices of religion. I am speaking of your own searching for a relationship with God, your Creator. The Bible states, "Then you will call upon Me and come and pray to Me, and I will listen to you. And you will seek Me and find Me when you search for Me with all your heart." (Jeremiah 29:12,13). And, when you know who you are in God, you can find and use your talents and gifts to build up and help other people. You enrich your life and that of others too.

"We sometimes search in a human being for that which only God can fill."

Two Single Thoughts to Consider
- *What do you truly want or need in an intimate relationship?*
- *What do you have to offer another person in an intimate relationship?*

Dating in the New World

A year or so after my divorce, I realized no one was going to come to my door and hand me my new life or a new relationship. My exposure to potential dates was very limited, so I decided to try Internet dating. If indeed I was going to venture out, I wanted to venture as far as I safely could. I figured the Internet was a step up from a bar or other social settings, yet it required an equal measure of guts and precaution. In reaching beyond my social circle, I entered into other worlds and cultures. In addition to meeting those with backgrounds similar to mine, I met many interesting and different people.

I discovered the richness of the French culture, the Jewish faith, and the Muslim heritage. None of these individuals would have come into my life without my stepping out of my comfort zone. How intriguing and fascinating people are if you will make yourself available to knowing them. Obviously, not every one of those relationships worked out, or my book would have a different title.

But I learned, as you will (or maybe already have) to trust my gut and learn from my mistakes. I've made plenty of mistakes. Being totally honest with yourself is the key. You'll get it right, just keep trying and learning from these beneficial mistakes. And don't marry them! Take your time - pay particular attention to those red flags that wave at you. Rely on the wisdom of your gut, that small voice that senses something is not right.

"How intriguing and fascinating people are if you will make yourself available to knowing them."

People Come into Your Life for a Reason

People come into your life for a reason, and they can bring many lessons with them. We can learn a lot about ourselves and our relationships, even the wrong ones.

Among my lessons, I learned that a healthy relationship consists of respect, honor, consideration, and acting upon mutual needs. I discovered that in a relationship, respect was so vital that I would not and could not do without it. You've probably already had some similar insights about what is essential in a relationship based on your past experiences.

Being with other personalities taught me about my own. It helped me pinpoint areas where I needed to grow as a person, and how much I had to learn about relationship dynamics. My new relationships, even those that were short lived, helped me clarify what I wanted, what I did not want, and what was unacceptable.

"I discovered that in a relationship, respect was so vital that I would not and could not do without it."

Dating Precautions

In Internet dating, I used several safety guidelines: the person I was corresponding with had to have posted a picture. If there was no photo, I would not respond, figuring that if they were really serious about an honest relationship they would identify themselves. I evaluated their written profile, looking for intelligent expression such as correctly spelled words. I compared their list of interests against mine. I did my best to determine if this person would be interesting and authentic and matched what I was looking for.

We would begin by emailing back and forth for a period of time, and if things clicked, we would talk on the phone. From there, we would arrange a brief meeting (coffee or a glass of wine) in a public place. I recommend that you let someone know where you are going and the name of the person you are meeting, even if it's only a first name and email address. When the date was over, I would call my friend to check in. I'm sure you agree, it's best to play it safe, especially in the beginning.

First Date Dynamics

I like to be a good listener, especially on a first date. I ask a lot of questions and let my date do most of the talking. I listen carefully because I want to know this person and get to the core of who he is. By observing and listening to the person, in my own way I exert control over the situation. It also makes me a good conversationalist in his eyes. He provides the information I need, such as his values, his philosophies on life, his preferences and it helps me decide if I want to pursue the relationship beyond a first meeting.

"When we were young and naïve, we didn't realize the complexity of relationships. Things seemed simpler, but they were also more superficial."

Dating is Different the Second Time Around

When we were young and naïve, we didn't realize the complexity of relationships. Things seemed simpler, but they were also more superficial. Now, as an adult, we need to consider the details of someone's past. Are they healed? Are they angry? Are they in a hurry to create a relationship?

What are they looking for? Do they need rescuing or are they looking for someone to rescue? Do they need to prove themselves? Observe carefully, listen intently and read between the lines. That's one of the things your gut does best.

Dating Behavior and the Honesty Factor

In dating, be who you are and say who you are. There's a lot of freedom in honesty. Honesty removes pretense, assumptions, expectations and guesswork. It tells us where we stand. One of the highest compliments you can receive when dating is being told that you are exactly who you said you were. Honesty saves everyone a lot of time (and grief) and allows us to find authentic relationships. Like me, perhaps you want to find someone who truly loves you for who you are, not someone they can create.

"In dating, be who you are and say who you are. There's a lot of freedom in honesty."

Three Single Thoughts to Consider
- *If you were to write a profile on yourself for Internet dating, what would you write? How would you describe what you are looking for?*
- *What core traits are you looking for in a partner?*
- *Define in your own words what comprises a healthy, authentic relationship.*

It's important to remember that women typically

form emotional attachments faster than men. So, women may need to safeguard their hearts until the person earns their trust. We need to proceed with caution, regardless of the flowers, soft words, manners or good looks. Step back, take a realistic look at what you want and need in a relationship. Don't try to desperately force the fit. Don't feel as if this is your last chance at a relationship because that's just not true.

Slowly and systematically, you learn the intricate steps in creating healthy relationships, making healthy choices and choosing when to be vulnerable. There is a time for putting forth the effort to make a relationship, and there is a time to guard yourself against making a relationship.

It is possible to truly love someone and grow past the blocks of the past. I did learn to become vulnerable and open again and found healthy people who could love me exactly for who I am. Although vulnerability carries the potential of disappointment or hurt, it is the only way to create an honest relationship.

"Slowly and systematically, you learn the intricate steps in creating healthy relationships, making healthy choices and choosing when to be vulnerable."

Simply Revealing

Here are a few things I learned about life from the men I dated. In a relationship there are things we need or want to know about the heart of the person we are with. I learned how important this is while I was dating a man for several months. I kept sensing that something was lacking but I couldn't put my finger on it. So, I asked him to write me a paragraph about our relationship. Not a letter, not a book, just a paragraph. I wanted to know what he thought of our relationship and what he saw in it. Since he was an educated man, well versed in the English language, this should have been an easy request. But he refused to do it. He couldn't do it, because he didn't feel it.

I used this test twice when my gut told me something was lacking. Both times I received the same response. None. This wasn't a test as much as it was an indicator of where each man's heart was, and I got what I asked for. This was a huge red flag that taught me something crucial. If you don't have his heart, you don't have him. If you don't have his heart, no matter what else he has to offer, you don't want him. Why? Because you can't keep someone who really isn't there.

"If you don't have his heart, no matter what else he has to offer, you don't want him. Why? Because you can't keep someone who really isn't there."

I also used what I call the "breakfast table test." I ask myself these questions, "Is this the person I could sit across from at the breakfast table every day of my life in my rawest form (before coffee) and he in his rawest form? Could I do that for the rest of my life?" For me, these revealing questions clarified and answered a lot.

Lessons Learned from the Men I Dated

1. Intensity doesn't mean authenticity. Sometimes physical attraction can lead us to believe there is really

something there of substance or authenticity. Is it lust or love? It takes time for a relationship to prove its authenticity. Intensity wanes with time, authenticity doesn't.

2. The negatives are often positives in disguise. What didn't work out for me instead worked for me. The relationships that didn't work out were actually positives. This freed me to seek a truer relationship. Even if you are the one who was rejected, then you are free to move on, discover more of who you are and where you need to be in your life. You are free to be available for the one who may come into your life who will truly love you and you will love in return.

3. Insecurities cannot be the glue that holds a relationship together. This is a strong argument for going through your healing process so you can become a stronger and healthier person. When you become strong and independent, you attract like-minded people who have the potential for creating strong relationships.

4. You must be yourself, even if it means ending a relationship. Ask yourself if this person will really fit into your life. Ask yourself if you are merely trying to keep the peace or continue the relationship at all costs. Refuse to settle for less than what you dream of or deserve. Do not compromise who you are or what you believe for someone else. No person or relationship is worth the cost. Being alone is a better choice than losing yourself in a superficial

"Intensity wanes with time, authenticity doesn't."

relationship that doesn't actually exist.

5. He may be more in love with the idea of having someone, than he is in love with you. One of the greatest lessons I learned is that sometimes the relationship wasn't about me at all. It was about his life, his insecurities, his needing to have someone with him, his proving himself as a man. Some men and some women need to prove their worth by seeing themselves through another person's eyes. If you see this red flag waving, move on.

6. People whose wounds are fresh (the very suddenly single) are a shaky proposition, at best. This may even include you at this time, especially if you're still within your first year of transition. If you meet a newly single person, value yourself enough to put up boundaries. As a rule, avoid getting involved with newly separated or divorced people. They have a lot of healing to go through before they are ready to have a healthy relationship again. You're inviting heartache if you open yourself up to someone who cannot possibly be ready for an intimate relationship. I say this because I've been there. I know several others who were also there. It takes time to get your head on straight. Be patient. Work on yourself. Your willingness to read this far into this book shows that you believe in yourself enough to work toward healing.

7. Boundaries are more vital for you than for the other person. It's not that you're shutting someone out.

"He may be more in love with the idea of having someone, than he is in love with you."

Boundaries are for your protection and they reflect the respect that you have for yourself. I didn't start out with clearly defined boundaries, but as time went on I learned to honor and respect myself more by having defining limits and conditions. I learned to avoid getting involved too quickly. As a girlfriend so eloquently stated, "He wanted wonderful sex, while I thought he wanted wonderful me." Boundaries are important. If you are worth it, he will wait for you. If not, you are worth more than he deserves.

8. As mentioned in chapter two, the healing relationship may most likely be the first relationship you'll have after becoming suddenly single. What I call the healing relationship is an attempt on your part to fill the void and escape the pain through someone else. It's not a real or a healthy relationship because you are not healed yet, but since you have to start somewhere this may have to occur. But guard yourself (and the other person) by being as honest as you can about what the relationship is or is not.

"Boundaries are for your protection and they reflect the respect that you have for yourself."

9. Some of us are attracted to strong people so we don't have to be strong ourselves. This is true of both men and women. I have met some wonderful men who loved being with strong women. Eventually I realized that some of them were drawn to strong women because they preferred not to be strong themselves.

After becoming single, I had to become the strong

person in decision making, financial management, self-discipline, and making mature choices. I didn't want to do that for anyone else. Strength should be shared between two adults, with each one respecting the other for their respective strengths. I didn't always want to be the strong one in the relationship and you probably don't either. Without mutual respect, you would in time come to dislike and ultimately despise the person. This may sound harsh, but better to know it now so you can make good choices in your relationships.

10. There is an art to a good argument. Handling disagreements constructively and respectfully is critical in a relationship. If you cannot argue well, you cannot live well together and the relationship will have a hard time surviving. Either you will need to be willing to work on the art of disagreement, or realize neither of you will change. In that case decide to move on. Handling disagreements requires the maturity to listen to each other so you can validate, appreciate and accept each other's viewpoint. To listen does not mean that you agree or that you are being "set straight". Listening displays respect to your partner. It allows each of you to explain your viewpoint and honor your right to have one. Acknowledge what the other person says. Be empathetic to what your partner is saying. The hardest part about handling conflict is listening without judgment, listening without interrupting and arguing

"If you cannot argue well, you cannot live well together and the relationship will have a hard time surviving."

without malice.

11. You will go through some "experimental" relationships during the process of dating. You may find yourself exploring new worlds, different adventures, unfamiliar territory. You have a Harley? Ok, I can do leather. A ponytail? Maybe. So, you're a singer in a blues band? I can be a groupie! Experimental relationships may be okay to visit, but could you introduce these characters to your kids, have them over for Thanksgiving or live their lifestyle over time? The wrong relationship helps us to be clearer about what the right one is.

12. Know when it's time to leave. Whether experimental or the real thing, be aware in every relationship that you are connecting with people who have the potential to be hurt. Sometimes the kindest thing you can do is to break off a relationship when you know it's not leading anywhere, especially if the other party wants it to become long term and you don't. Let them go find someone who will love them in the way they want and need to be loved.

"The wrong relationship helps us to be clearer about what the right one is."

Dating Games

A couple of men I met on the Internet told me stories of some women who presented false fronts and played the "dating games." One woman posted a friend's picture instead of her own. Another used a ten-year old picture, while others exaggerated attributes and assets. But how long can such a charade last? The truth eventually comes out. The excitement of attention will quickly be overshadowed by the disappointment of rejection. It's ironic that these women played games when all they really wanted was someone who would love them for who they were. Artificial tactics may attract, but they won't keep. We could all save ourselves a good deal of time, energy and maybe even heartache if we were willing to be ourselves. Genuine love requires honesty. It's that simple and that foundational.

You will undoubtedly have your own "lessons learned" after you've dated a while. Things that are vital to you now perhaps weren't even a consideration the last time you dated. Listen to your gut even more than you listen to your heart.

"Artificial tactics may attract, but they won't keep. Genuine love requires honesty. It's that simple and that foundational."

Learning to Flirt

I sat at the bar in a nice restaurant with my wonderful girlfriend, Darcy, a wild, delightfully crazy friend who keeps me young. Darcy is a natural flirt. One night I asked her to teach me how to flirt. It was a comical conversation, reminiscent of high school times. Darcy said that when you flirt, you need to initiate by making direct eye contact, hold your gaze for five seconds, then look away. Repeat it. The process sounded really easy, but it was a bit beyond my comfort zone.

Darcy emphasized that it doesn't have to be a seductive stare, but simply an "I'm interested" look. I immediately tried looking at a nice looking man (who wore no ring), but three seconds into it I started giggling. I looked away embarrassed and tried again, but I giggled again. The poor guy must have thought I was laughing at him. Maybe flirting requires more than eye contact. I never did acquire the skill, but maybe you're more of a natural like Darcy.

Four Seasons

We can't know someone until we've seen him or her through every season and observe how they live through each one. In a year's time you will find out what happens when he gets mad, how he (or she) handles emergencies, how family members are treated and how restaurant servers or co-workers are handled. You will observe the traditions of family, how he reacts when the vending machine eats his quarters or the stock market devalues his investment. Values emerge during a year's time if you're observant enough to notice them.

Just like a race car driver, who by ignoring the red flags is putting his life at risk, your gut gives you red flags which you should heed. Be honest with yourself about the truth of your relationships. The issues that surface won't go away. If you think they will just disappear, think again.

"Be honest with yourself about the truth of your relationships. The issues that surface won't go away."

It is not a case of mind over matter. I know, because I've tried it. Those issues you rationalized away will resurface after you've truly opened your heart and made yourself vulnerable. Face them now, because denying their existence only postpones and eventually magnifies the problem to face at a later date. It's hard to be so brutally honest when you so desperately want things to work. But for the long-term salvation of your heart and your own well being, pay close attention to those red flags so you can move on to a healthy, right relationship.

Good or bad, you have to face the reality of the relationship. It may hurt now, but not nearly as much as it will down the road. Denial will not make the problem go away. That's why it is important to be strong and independent, so you have the courage to leave a bad situation. You'll be able to see the red flags waving and you won't deny that they are there.

"That's why it is important to be strong and independent, so you have the courage to leave a bad situation."

Three Single Thoughts to Consider
- *What is the biggest lesson you have learned from closely observing other relationships?*
- *If you are dating, what red flags have begun waving and what are you doing about them?*
- *Did you ignore red flags in any past relationships, and if so what lessons did you learn?*

"Don't cry because it ended, smile because it was."

Author Unknown

Why Some of us Become Cynical

It is amazing that after all our ups and downs that some of us remain hopeless romantics. But others become cynical. Cynicism is the living out of anger or injustice. It displays itself in our attitude. Cynicism is a form of self-protection, an attempt to avoid hurt. Yes the hurt was real, a trust was broken and a hard shell now encases what was once an open heart.

Investing in a relationship includes building expectations for what we believe is a future. As we invest and drop our defenses, we make assumptions that may or may not be true. If we get burned or taken advantage of, or hurt because we let ourselves be vulnerable, we can become cynical. We may tuck it into our emotional pocket to continually refer to. Cynicism can harden your heart and become more powerful than it ought. Don't be angry because you opened yourself up to someone. It's called the vulnerability of being human and the risk of loving. And maybe Alfred Lord Tennyson was right after all, "Tis better to have loved and lost, than to never have loved at all."

"It is amazing that after all our ups and downs that some of us remain hopeless romantics."

If You are Really Serious

To find the perfect person is impossible, because no

174

one is perfect. Yes, that includes you and me. But there are some questions that can help clarify what's perfect for you. If you are really serious about a relationship or starting to date, here are some questions to ponder.

- Does this person honor me in our relationship?
- Does the person ask my opinion and respect my input?
- Would this person be there for me if I lost the capacity to function in areas of health, finances or emotions?
- Would this person choose me as a priority over their friends?
- Does this person love my children?
- Does this person value my body?
- How does this person handle my sensitivities?
- How does he value the women in his life (Mother, daughter, and sister)?

"Set your standards high. If this forces you to be alone for a longer period, then at least you'll be alone with dignity and inner peace."

No, you aren't looking for the "perfect" mate. But you know that the person you love will be a reflection of who you are, how you feel about yourself and what you want for the future. You want the best for yourself and for the one you choose to love. Look for the perfect person for you. Set your standards high. If this forces you to be alone for a longer period, then at least you'll be alone with dignity and inner peace.

Adventures of the Heart

"The heart has its reasons that reason knows not of."

Blaise Pascal

Relationships are not an exact science, nor can they ever be. We can never totally understand or fully comprehend what we really want or need in a relationship. But there are wonderful lessons to learn about the whys and the wherefores. I had the privilege to learn some of these lessons while getting to know some wonderful people. The men I dated taught me a lot about myself. They showed me my strengths and they showed me my weaknesses. Most importantly, they made me be honest with myself about what was essential for me in a relationship. They also taught me about life in so many ways.

Through their eyes and through their worlds I was exposed to adventures I would have never experienced on my own. I had the opportunity to be proposed to and to be let down lightly, and given the opportunities to know when it was time to leave.

There was the man who adored me to the point of smothering, and the man who truly loved me and wanted to marry me. There was the man who transformed my living room into a romantic dance floor. There were men who showed me the world, introduced me to cultures, languages and brilliant conversation. There was a man that taught me

"Relationships are not an exact science, nor can they ever be. We can never totally understand or fully comprehend what we really want or need in a relationship."

that I truly could fall in love with someone. I met men who were gorgeous on the outside and men who were gorgeous on the inside, men with issues, men who lied and told fanciful stories, men who created instant attraction but lacked substance. I met those who showed me their heart and those who never could, men who only wanted to play and men who had forgotten how to play.

I met men who were still searching for themselves and their dreams, even though their hair was turning gray. And I found men who will always be my dear friends and nothing more. I can't imagine my life without them. But what they all taught me, most of all, is that I must make my own life, find my own peace and create my own happiness.

"What they all taught me, most of all, is that I must make my own life, find my own peace and create my own happiness."

There were relationships that I wished had gone on longer than they did and some I let go on for too long. This is the world of dating, from marriage proposals to broken hearts. There are no guarantees, no way to keep your heart fully safe, but I learned to dig deep to know these men. I learned to savor and live every moment with each person because sometimes relationships end unexpectedly and only then do we realize we didn't savor the experience or the person quite enough.

Take the Risk in Relationships

I don't know where you come from or what scars or

fears you carry from past relationships, but in your dating adventures you'll meet those who will think you are the most wonderful person in the world. Others will look right past you. But prepare yourself to meet some wonderful people. Be open to the possibilities, and be prepared to seek out the opportunities to meet new people. Your presence will add to their lives as well.

They will intrigue you, fascinate you and at times frustrate you. Some of the people you meet will treat you like royalty, others a pauper. Maybe you'll try the paragraph test or the breakfast table test, as you attempt to reveal the truth. You'll need to be strong enough to face the truth when it surfaces.

You will find your own methods for seeking the truth from your gut, for setting boundaries and teaching yourself not to settle. In each dating relationship, ask questions, even the obvious ones, so you can know as much as possible about where you fit in and if this person is a good fit for you. For now, and for always, you must first come to grips with that person you see in the mirror. You have to love yourself fully and unconditionally before you can give that kind of love to anyone else. You deserve to be loved for exactly who you are, not someone that the other person needs you to be, or someone you think you must create.

"You deserve to be loved for exactly who you are, not someone that the other person needs you to be, or someone you think you must create."

Don't Settle

Lessons learned are the by-products and the gifts that come out of relationship adventures. Don't settle into a relationship until you find what your gut and your head agree is the mate for you. Try being best friends first. Strive, early on, for a strong friendship instead of a romantic relationship. Go ahead and be that hopeless romantic, but also live your life passionately in other areas. Pursue your own interests, dreams and goals. Don't wait for the perfect relationship to change your life.

"Go ahead and be that hopeless romantic, but also live your life passionately in other areas. Don't wait for the perfect relationship to change your life."

Although you and I may secretly long for that wonderful relationship and keep our eyes open for it, we can't let it be the consuming focus of our value and significance. A loving relationship means different things to each of us. How clearly can you define what love means to you? Does it include total acceptance, a future, tenderness, respect, and passion? What behaviors and what actions support your definition? Perhaps in the quietest of moments you've begun defining the kind of relationship you want in your future. And that if you don't get what you want, being single will work out just fine.

Go into a relationship without expectations, as much as possible. Enjoy and appreciate who they are and who you are independently. Be honest with yourself, even if it hurts. Don't let your life or level of happiness be determined by the relationship you're in because if it ends so does your foundation. Nourish all of your relationships, honor all people and realize relationships are not the ultimate and only answer to your happiness. The greatest relationship is first with your God and then with yourself.

"The greatest relationship is first with your God and then with yourself."

Chapter 9

Taking On The World And Making It Yours

Perspective is everything.

You have begun one of life's most difficult transitions. Consider how far you've come since the very first moments. The persistence that has brought you to the last chapter of this book will keep you going to the new life you want to start. Your persistence and determination will expand your world and all the potential your future holds. You can live this new life, and you can live it well. I have known people who blossom after this major event in their life, and those who emotionally wither and die inside. You can be the one who surprises many, (including yourself) to emerge stronger than you ever thought possible, and to live a life more meaningful and wonderful than you ever dreamed existed. As you look at each new day with the fading intensity of the past, visualize your future. You can pronounce that you were bigger than this crisis and that you rose to face the challenges. You can note that while the past has hurt you, it did not defeat you. This is your powerful and individual choice.

> *"The persistence that has brought you to the last chapter of this book, will keep you going to the new life you want to start."*

Living All The Days Of Your Life

Perspective is everything. It is not what happens to you, it's how you react to it and your perspective that makes all the difference. I hope by now you may have some clarity on the direction where you want your life to go. And I hope you have written out your dreams and the definition of what a successful life is to you, because remember, you have to be the one to define it. It takes strength to reconstruct your life, faith to survive this transition, hard work to redefine what's important and then to work on what really matters. If you make this transition with determination and focus, you will most likely find what is really important is actually very short, and your definition of success becomes very simple and more authentic.

"It is not what happens to you, it's how you react to it and your perspective that makes all the difference."

You may find the definition of success is not elusive at all, but is found within the very basics of life. I did. For me, it is my relationship with God and those I love. Undoubtedly, you will discover who your true family is and who your real friends are as you travel through this transition. You will see those who stick by you through your toughest times. You will never forget their kindness and you will cherish them for a lifetime. Through the process of divorce or the death of a mate, you will discover that no man or woman is an island. You and I need other people in our lives and we need to contribute to the lives of others to give our life meaning. Start pursuing authentic friendships that provide a heart to heart relationship, and put forth the effort to go beyond a superficial level. Do not withdraw and keep to yourself right now, you will miss out and deny yourself the rewards of relationships. Be proactive in creating your network of friends. Seek out people who are emotionally healthy and who provide positive reinforcement for who you want to become. Ask yourself if the relationships you have now fill these values.

Redefining your life takes honesty and it takes courage; courage to step out toward a new world you're redesigning, and courage to step inside and create new beliefs to shift the paradigm that has been true for so many years. Create a new perspective that being single can be strong and whole, and then begin to act on that perspective. To succeed in being single is to grow through this transition and see it as an opportunity for wonderful personal change. It is a transition within the heart.

"Create a new perspective that being single can be strong and whole, and then begin to act on that perspective."

"There is no shortcut to life. To the end of our days, life is a lesson imperfectly learned."

Harrison Salisbury

Pivotal Actions to make a new life

If you could take just three pivotal actions from this book to assist you in the transition into a new life, I encourage you to;

1) Strengthen the presence of God in your life to keep you grounded.
2) Be conscious of the quality of the decisions you make; they determine your future.
3) Be open and willing to take intelligent risks into your future.

These three points, along with accentuating your life with a network of friends, will facilitate your transition into creating a successful life.

First - the importance of God is multidimensional. Finding God is for stability. The scriptures are real. They are solid and foundational to life. Their principles will never change and they can level out the roller coaster of emotions. They will guide you and give you direction. They supply comfort, hope, and confidence in your present trying times and your future. They will underscore your value, regardless of what any former spouse may have said. I emerged from my divorce emotionally torn up and physically worn down. Even though I knew of God's love for me, by Bible and verse, I was amazed at how personal He became during this time. I witnessed how He met so many of my needs by demonstrating His love and care for me. I opened the Bible again, this time opening myself up to it more desperately and personally and willing to grasp the true value that God places on me. I believe Jesus to be the Son of God and that his death is proof of that love and the pathway to an intimate relationship with God. When I grasped that more clearly, I came to understand that His love for me gives me incredible value, and I will never doubt my worth or significance again. I pray that you have discovered that.

Second - make wise decisions during this powerful time of transition. Your decisions will affect the rest of your life. This is true in every area, from the emotional to the financial. When I left the big house in the country, though difficult, it was a wise decision. By making solid decisions you will overcome your newly found insecurities and become more confident in the decisions you make. You will learn to follow your gut. As you become more comfortable accepting life in a single perspective your decision-making skills will become stronger. You may decide you actually like being on your own after all. You can find peace within your decisions because you've found peace within yourself. You are reaching inward for that peace instead of outward and finding fulfillment in ways other than an exclusive relationship. This is a critical time for wise decisions. Pay attention to the "big picture" of your future. Your decisions have ramifications to those around you, especially your children. Your decisions can make or break your relationship with them and influence their level of respect for you for the rest of their lives. This is a powerful

"You may decide you actually like being on your own after all. You can find peace within your decisions because you've found peace within yourself."

and fragile time. Your decisions profoundly matter because you will live with the results of your choices for a very long time, if not the rest of your life.

Third - your willingness to take risks is vital as you lay the foundation of your future. Calculated risks force us to grow, and to become more confident. To risk is to step out, to have faith in yourself, and to believe in your future. It takes hard work to try new things and to open yourself up to new ideas and possibilities that may not work out. But every successful life requires risks of some sort. Elbert Hubbard said it well, " The greatest mistake you can make in life is to be continually fearing you will make one." You will never know what you are missing, nor can you make life an adventure unless you try something new. Be willing to stretch yourself, and don't always be predictable. Evaluate your options and take action, which will involve taking risks. If you don't succeed the first time, claim the lesson and remember it. Be kind to yourself and smile at your mistakes. It means you're human, like the rest of us. Don't let past mistakes keep you from trying something new. When you step outside of your comfort zone, congratulate yourself for your willingness to try. As the Chinese proverb states "Fall down seven times, get up eight." Take the risk of living fully so you know you've experienced life and not merely responded to it. Take life beyond your present world into greater experiences and deeper knowledge.

"This is a powerful and fragile time. Your decisions profoundly matter because you will live with the results of your choices for a very long time, if not the rest of your life."

Proclaim to yourself, "I am grateful that today is mine and I will find cause to celebrate my life." Buy yourself some flowers instead of waiting for someone else to do it. Or buy yourself a single rose, to symbolize the passion you have for your newly single life.

Risk by opening yourself up to what's new. Look up, look out and expand your world. There is too much to do, too many worlds to explore, and too many fascinating people to meet. In your current life, you have people who care about you, love you, and want you to succeed. There are new people you'll meet in the future who will do the same. Someone in the world is waiting to meet you and they need you in their life as much as you need them in yours. Step out! Live life beyond the everyday routines and take heart in all you see before you.

"Step out! Live life beyond the everyday routines and take heart in all you see before you."

Grab your dreams with both hands and a bold heart. Shake off the negativity of the past so you can find your new spirit. Take the good lessons the past has given you and let them help you head toward your new future.

A broken heart is a tender teacher about the preciousness of love and the fragility of life - embrace your lessons by living life fully and not wasting any days. Time is precious and fleeting.

Three Single thoughts To Consider

- *What vital action into your new life do you need to take now?*
- *How might it influence and change your future?*
- *How will you hold yourself accountable to live your life fully as its own celebration each day?*

Create Your New Life of Passion

"Your life was never meant to be ordinary. It is meant to be lived passionately."

Passion is defined as "boundless enthusiasm, the object of such love or desire; an abandoned display of emotions." To be passionate means to be capable of experiencing powerful positive emotions. Connect with your passion. Find that love and inner drive and rekindle the things that excite you, the things you may have forgotten with the stresses of life. Where is your passion? Uncover it, explore it, and start living it. From hobbies, intellectual pursuits, to outdoor activities or some other creative quests; get your juices flowing. Whatever you pursue, whether it be grand or small, recognize that passion enriches your life. Connect your passions to the dreams of your future and how you want your life to be. Awaken your curiosity. Your life was never meant to be ordinary. It is meant to be lived passionately.

The Upside of Being Single

There are many good sides to being single. I have

discovered one great part of being single is the freedom I enjoy and the tighter control over my own life. And now is the time to find your joy in being single. Marvel at the new dynamics in your life, full of opportunity to renew you. Take note of the changes that can be exciting for you, choose the perspective to look at the things that are full in your life and not the things that may be empty or missing. For the suddenly single, accountability takes on a whole new meaning.

- You are accountable to your God, your conscience, and to your family in a whole new way.
- You can control your finances adding freedom and power to your life. Being fiscally responsible gives you confidence in the present and in your future.
- You can create your own peace, the turmoil of this transition is over. You have more control over your life than you ever had. There is no one arguing or disapproving. Peace is priceless.
- You will have more time to spend in creative ways, such as volunteering for a good cause. What is your favorite charity? The women's shelter, your church, the PTO, fundraiser for a park project? What about a mission's trip? Seek fulfillment in serving other people's needs. It will refresh you and fill your life with wonderful things, including the self-fulfillment you may be searching for. Refresh yourself by refreshing others

"Marvel at the new dynamics in your life, full of opportunity to renew you."

and in helping them find their dreams.

- Time to go after your own interests, (theatre, pottery, book club, soccer team, night classes)

- Time to play, stay out late, go to band concerts, (the ones you've missed in high school or college). Try the opera for the first time. How about breakfast at midnight with a friend? This could be a liberating time for you. And being single could lessen the obligation of cooking square meals. Will the kids mind if you have peanut butter and jelly or cereal for dinner once in a while? Make it balanced, but make it simple. What's the good part of the new household now? Get creative with cooking, exactly how you want it. Is it cheese and tomato sandwiches? Crab dip and crackers with a glass of wine? Make it as extravagant or as simple as you wish; scallops in wine sauce. Where is that recipe book? You can make larger portions and phone a friend to share it with you. Food is the great socializer!

"Embrace the peace and the freedom to redesign your life inside and out. You have a new slate and a new start."

- Housework can make changes to new duties and new delegations. Be creative, you can decide to take a morning run or clean the house that morning. Change the routines to suit you and your household. Embrace the peace and the freedom to redesign your life inside and out. You have a new slate and a new start.

- Make new traditions for the holidays. Keep the favorite

ones of the past, but make new traditions to mark your new life. It will allow you to find hope through the holidays of transition, and new traditions offer more reasons to celebrate.

Reach In, Reach Out

Compensate for not having a "relationship" by having lots of relationships. It is scientifically proven that those with intimate relationships get sick less often, heal faster, and live longer than those who don't. Create your network by initiating a day out with friends. Don't wait to be asked, make the first move. Ask someone to join you for a movie and dinner. Surprise someone with a favor. Buy chocolate for your department at work. Nurture friendships by being a good friend. Send a card or make a homemade gift. Bless yourself by giving to others and delighting in their reaction. Cultivate relationships that are a positive influence in your life, ones that build you up and encourage you. As you heal and become more whole, you will find that you don't have the energy for unhealthy relationships. Set boundaries, so you can let go of the people who aren't good for you. Love them, but let them go. Find positive, intelligent people to hang out with. Become the person that others want to be around. Redefine your relationships, deepen your connections and create a new authentic deep bond with those you care about.

"Bless yourself by giving to others and delighting in their reaction. Become the person that others want to be around."

Maybe your path will never include the man or woman of your dreams. That does not mean life won't be wonderful and full of incredible adventures out there for you. Go and live your life in extraordinary style as you are single. Your world is full of possibilities and there is no way to predict the future. Live your life as a whole person. Live life on purpose and at the same time live it lightly, not taking things too seriously or sweating the minutia that bogs you down. Find some fun friends to keep you vibrant and alive. Learn from their interesting perspectives and insights. Rediscover the joy of laughter and remind yourself to laugh. Make a sign and hang it in your kitchen if you must, but find the time to laugh. Be open to the new, the different, and the intriguing. Rediscover the eccentric and those who have extreme views. They will either authenticate your own views, or open you up to new ideas.

"Rediscover the joy of laughter and remind yourself to laugh."

Single Mindedness

Where do you go from here? Will you empower yourself to live a successful life? Maybe there isn't anything new you haven't seen before within these pages. However, the right idea at the right time can inspire you to act. That is the purpose of this book- to inspire you to act, to move into your greatest adventure, your greatest life, and it begins now.

It is a strange way to come to this place in your life, but this is where you are. Accept what is, accept where you are and make it beautiful. Go after your own life with all the enthusiasm it deserves. The future is there for you to approach, to confront, to experience. If you stop to truly think about it, more choices stand before you now than ever before. No one owes you a living, but you owe yourself a life. By taking some practical approaches to this new life, the single life can be a wonderful one. You can find joy again. You can smile, laugh, cherish and love those near to you. Who knows, after a time of healing you may even fall in love again. But don't wait for it, start your life now. As you begin this powerful time in making your new life, accept the new challenges along with the gift of every moment. By finding yourself suddenly single, you may just discover that you are suddenly loving it!

"Accept where you are and make it beautiful."